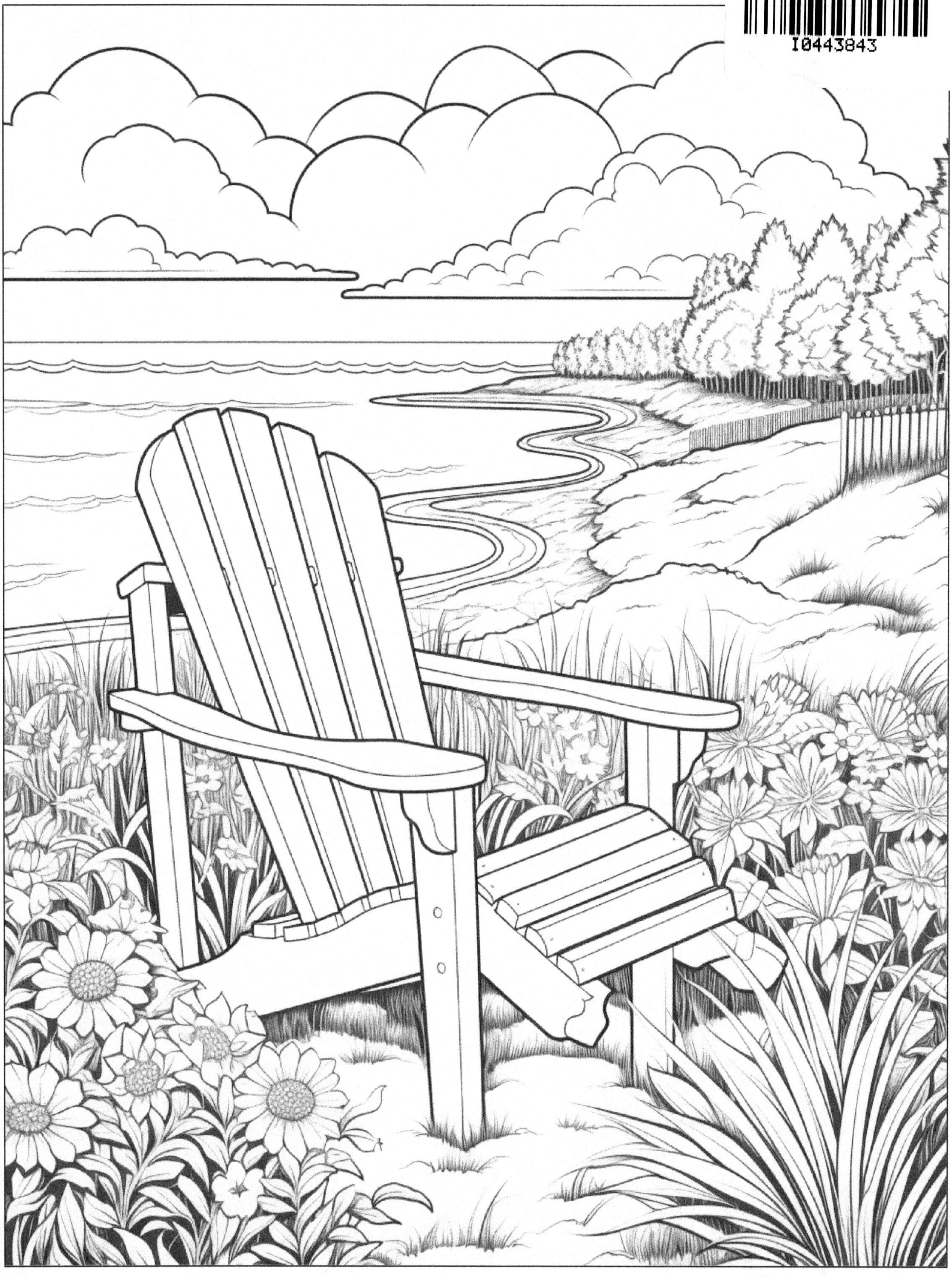

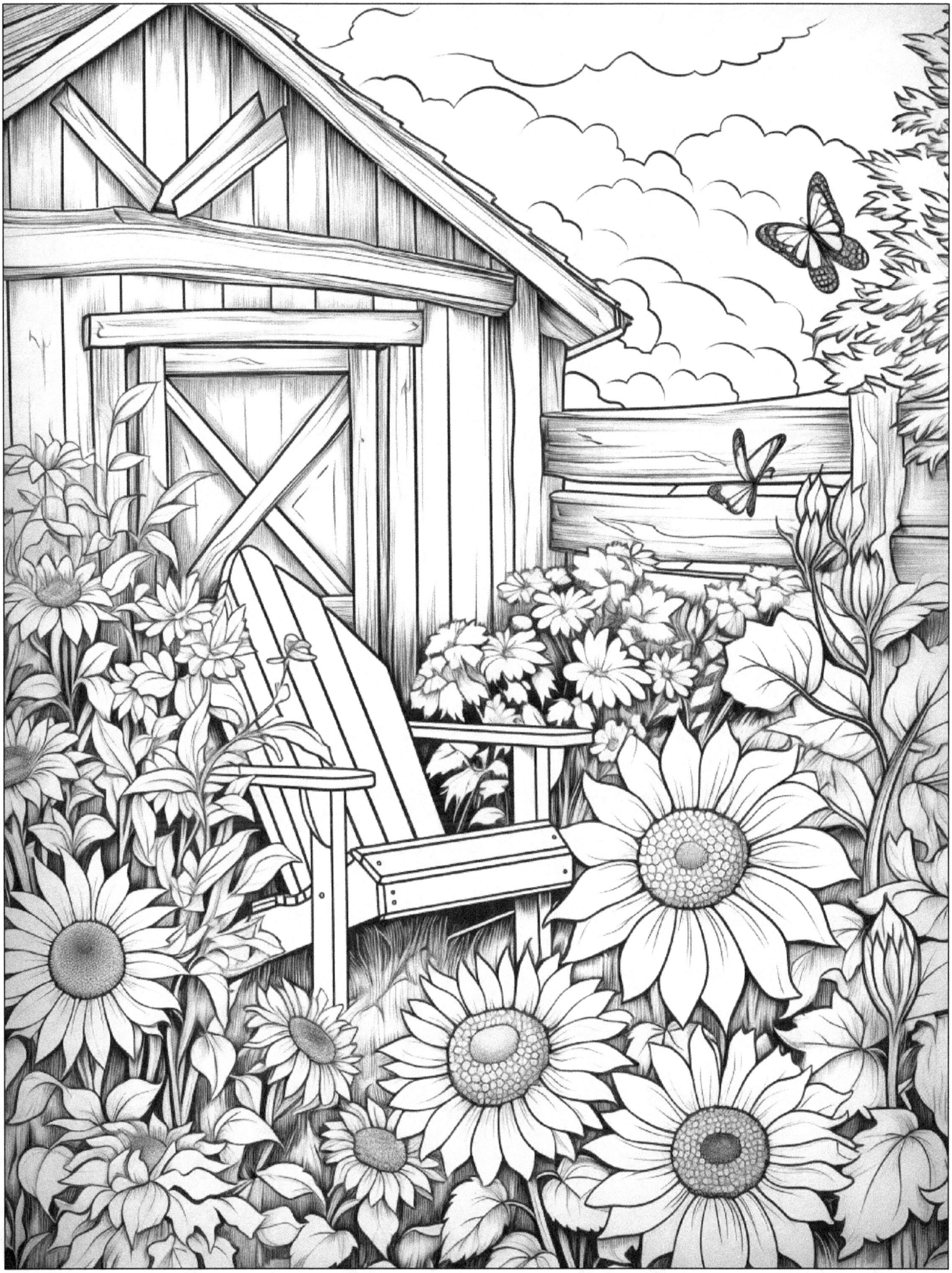

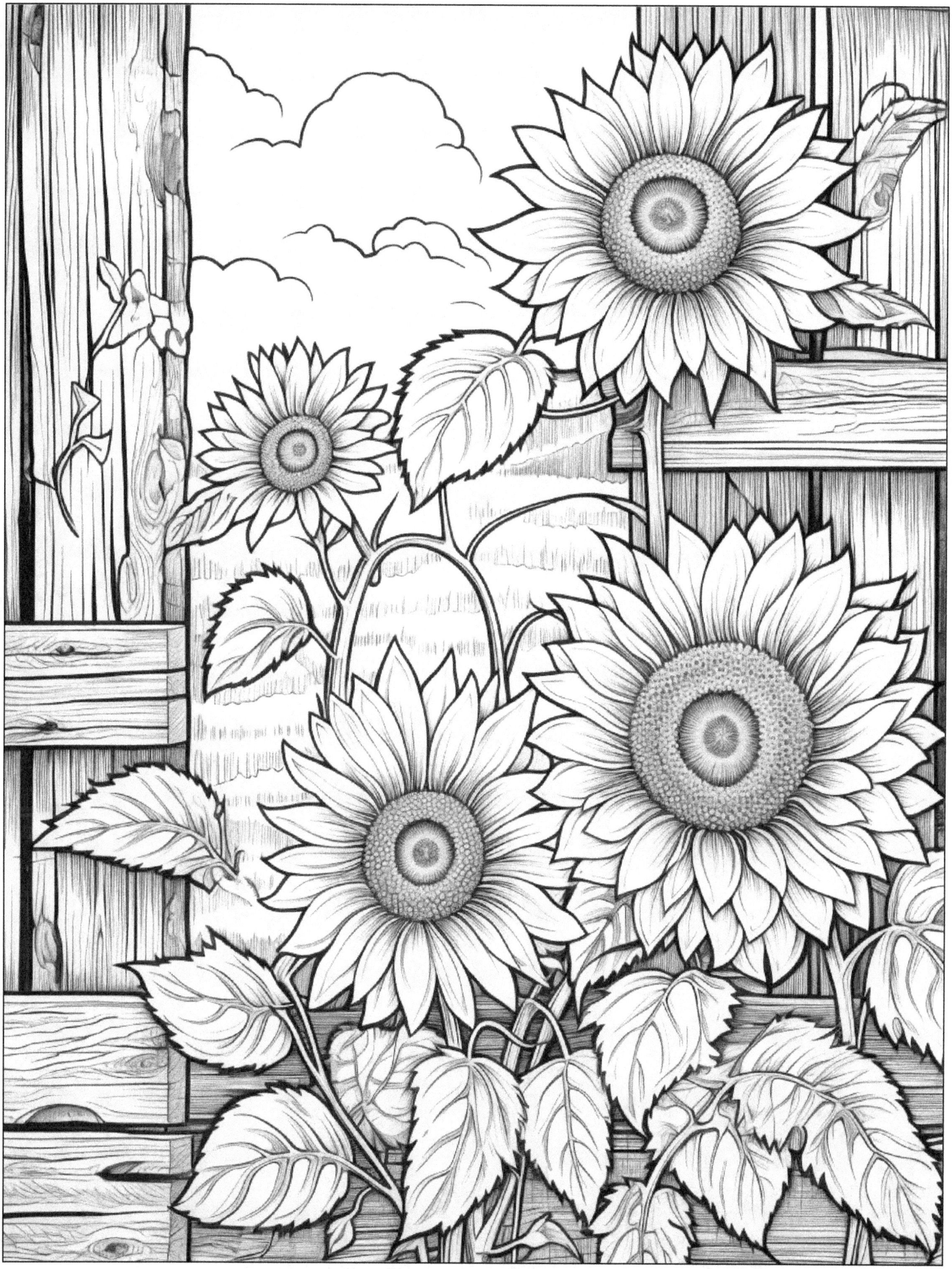

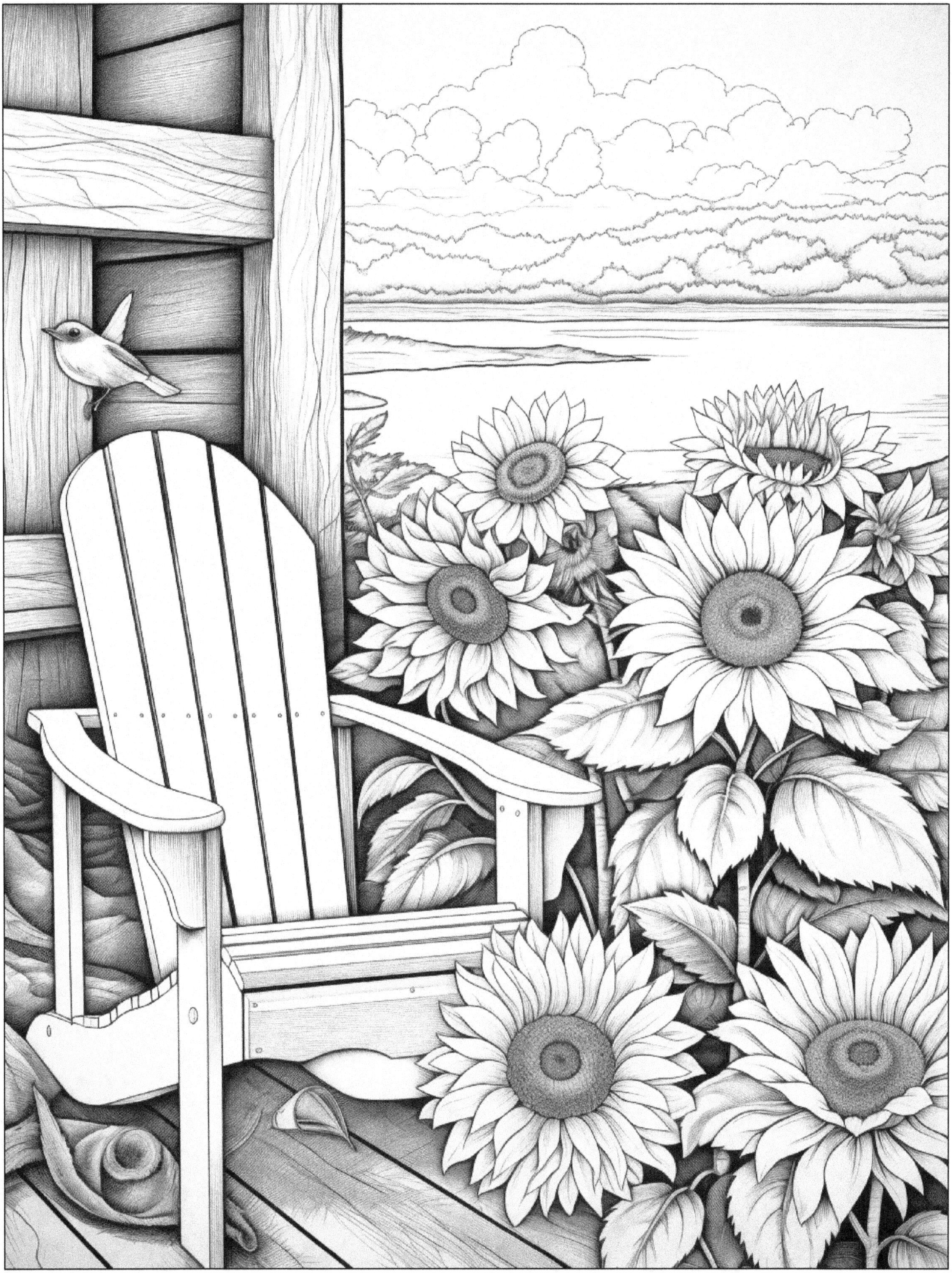

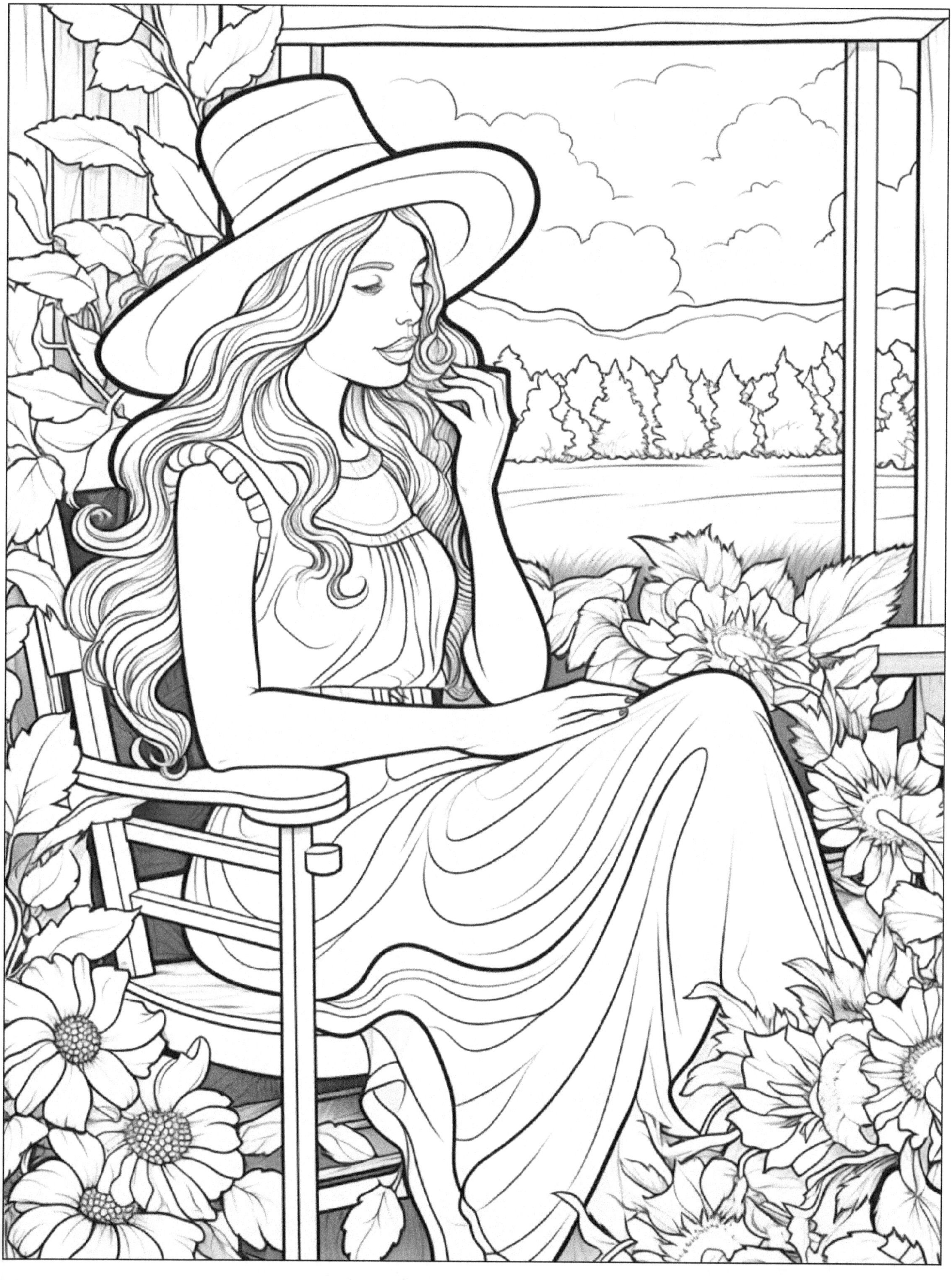

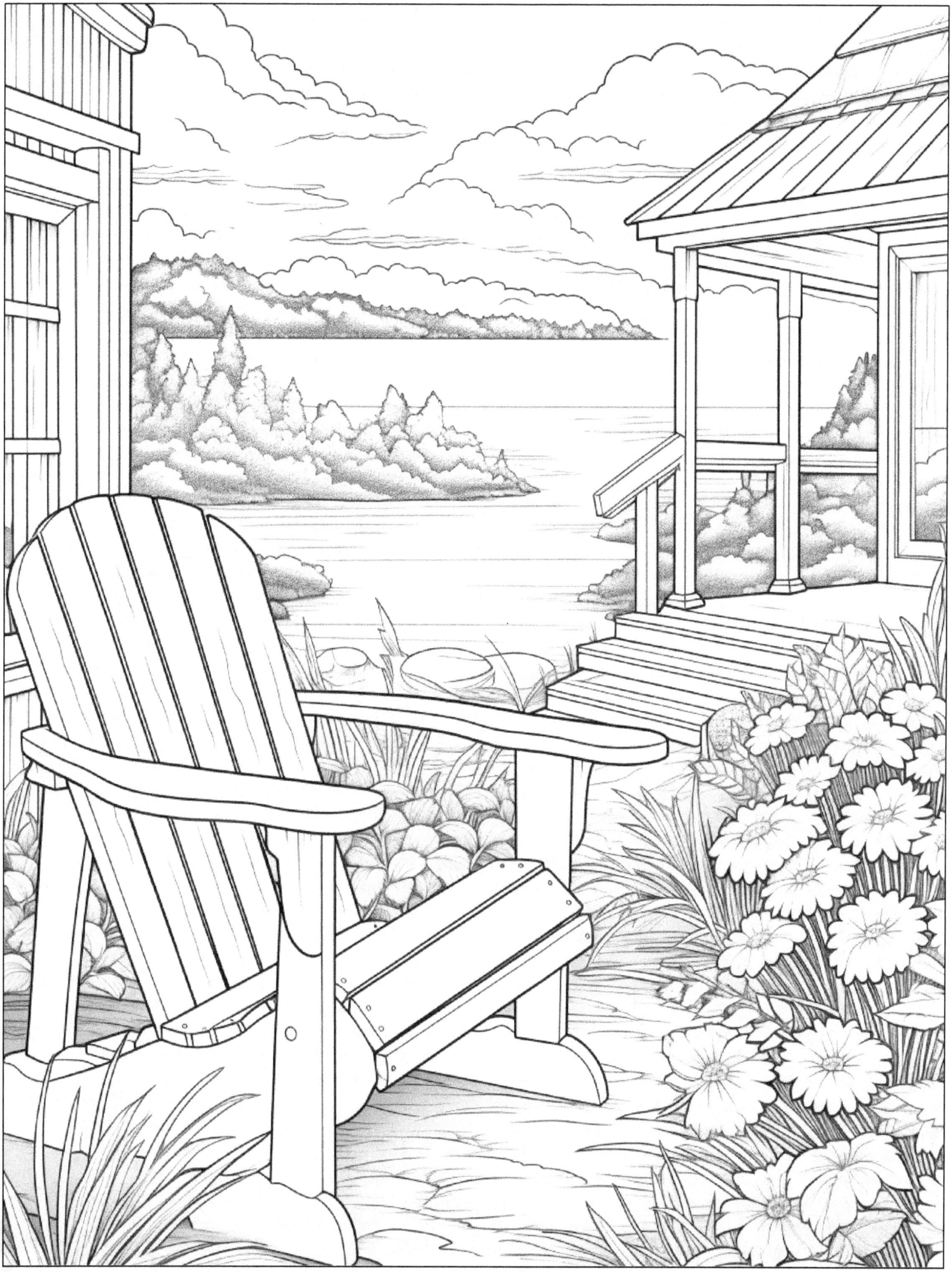

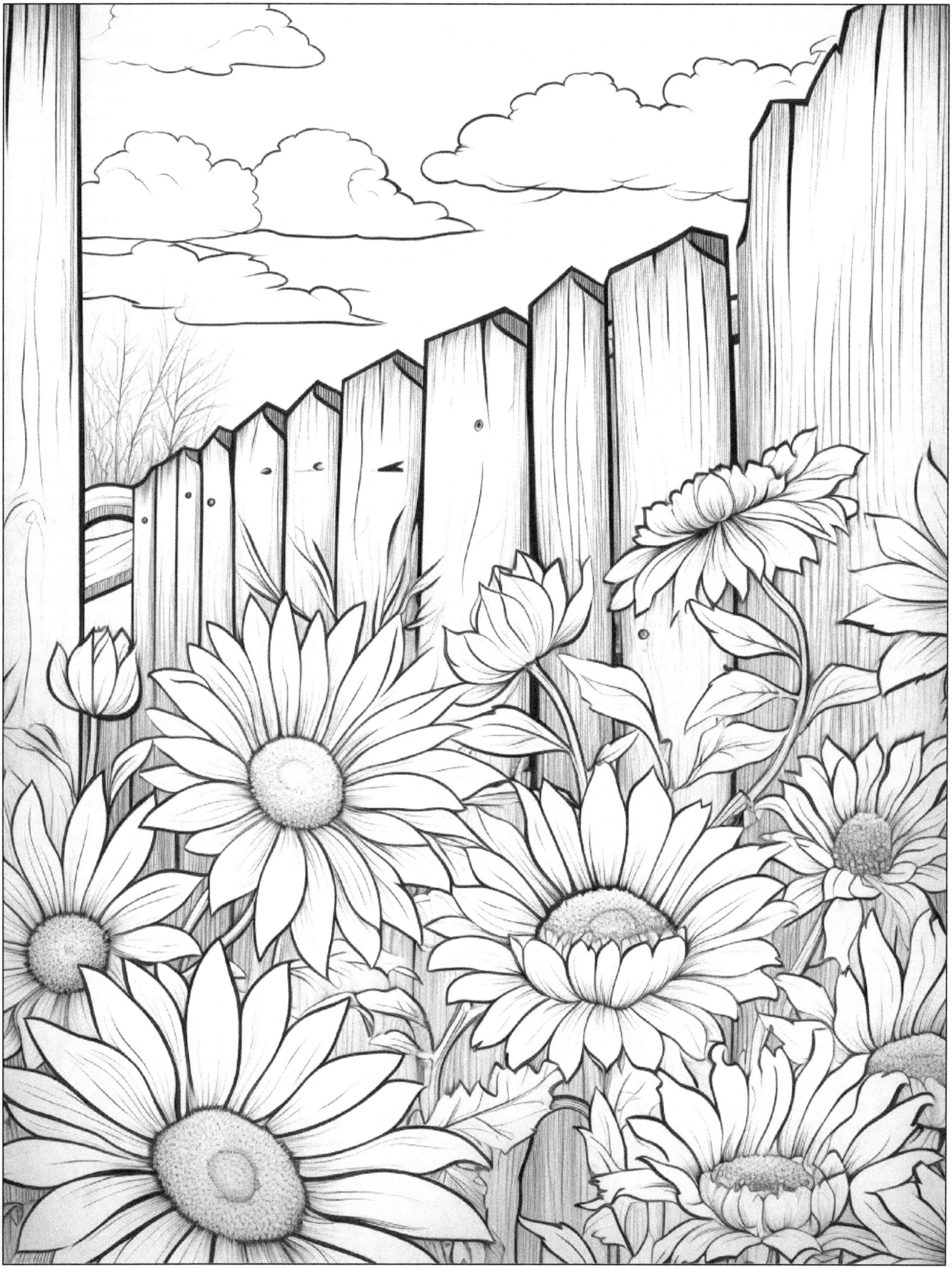

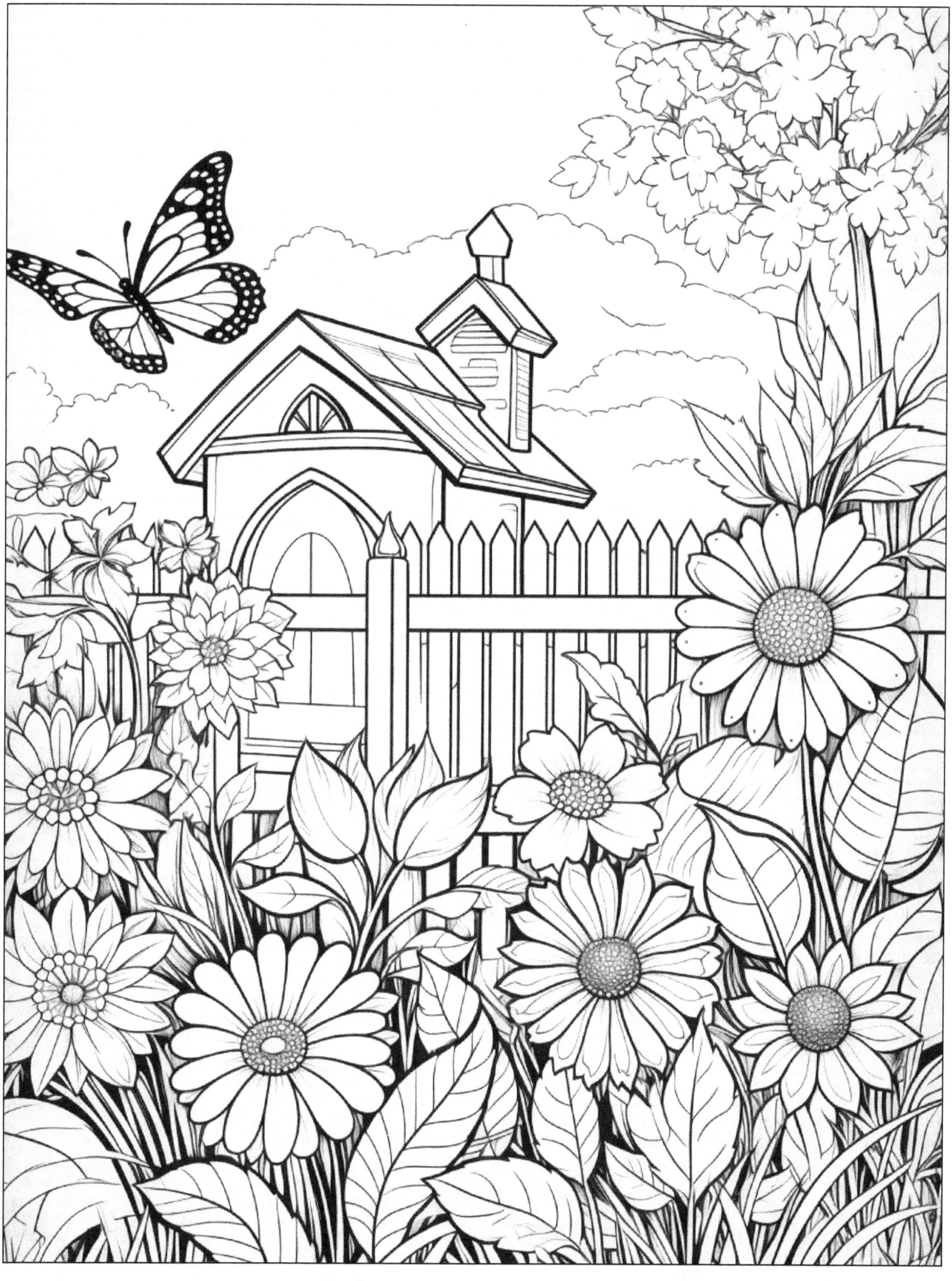

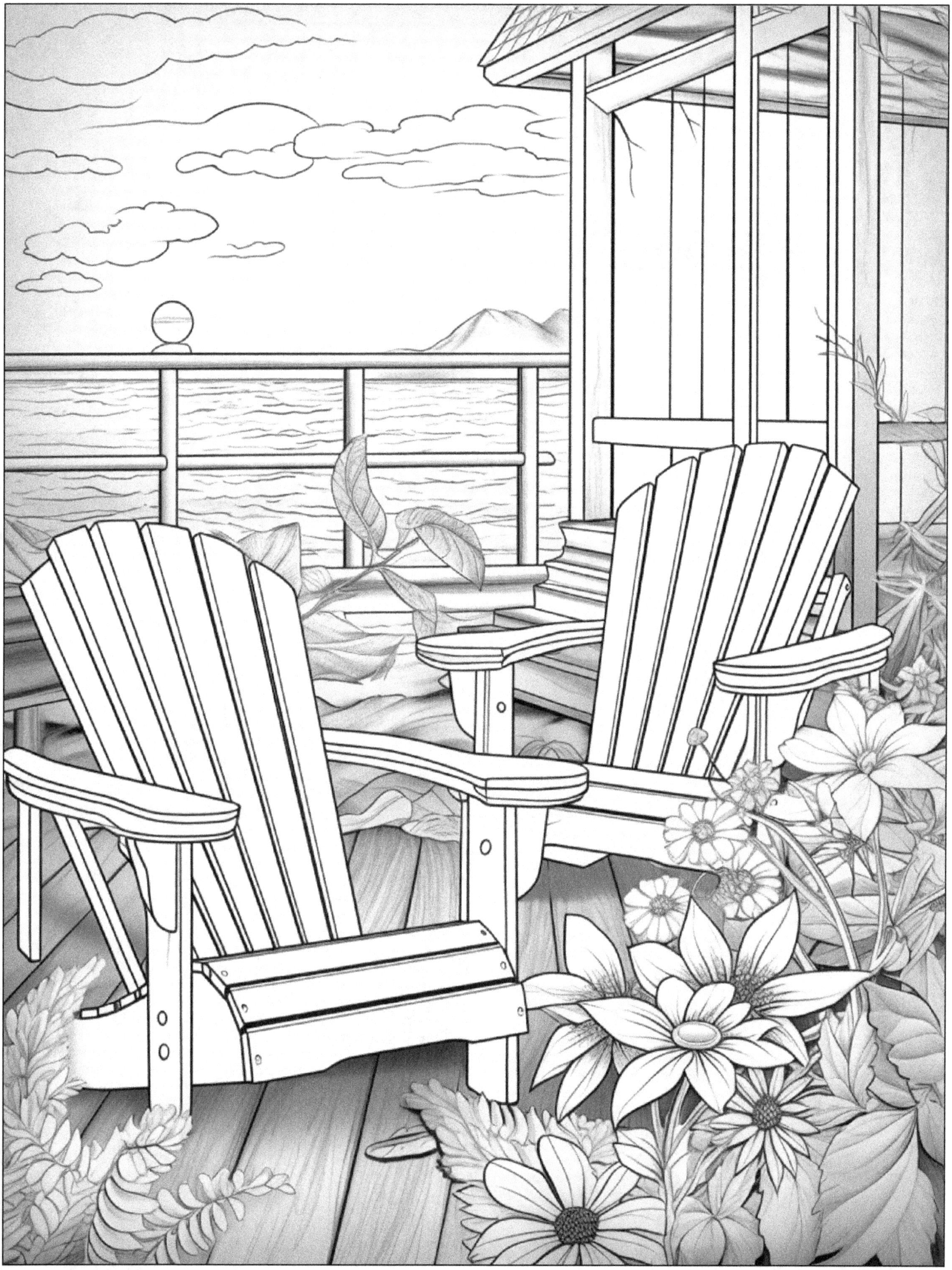

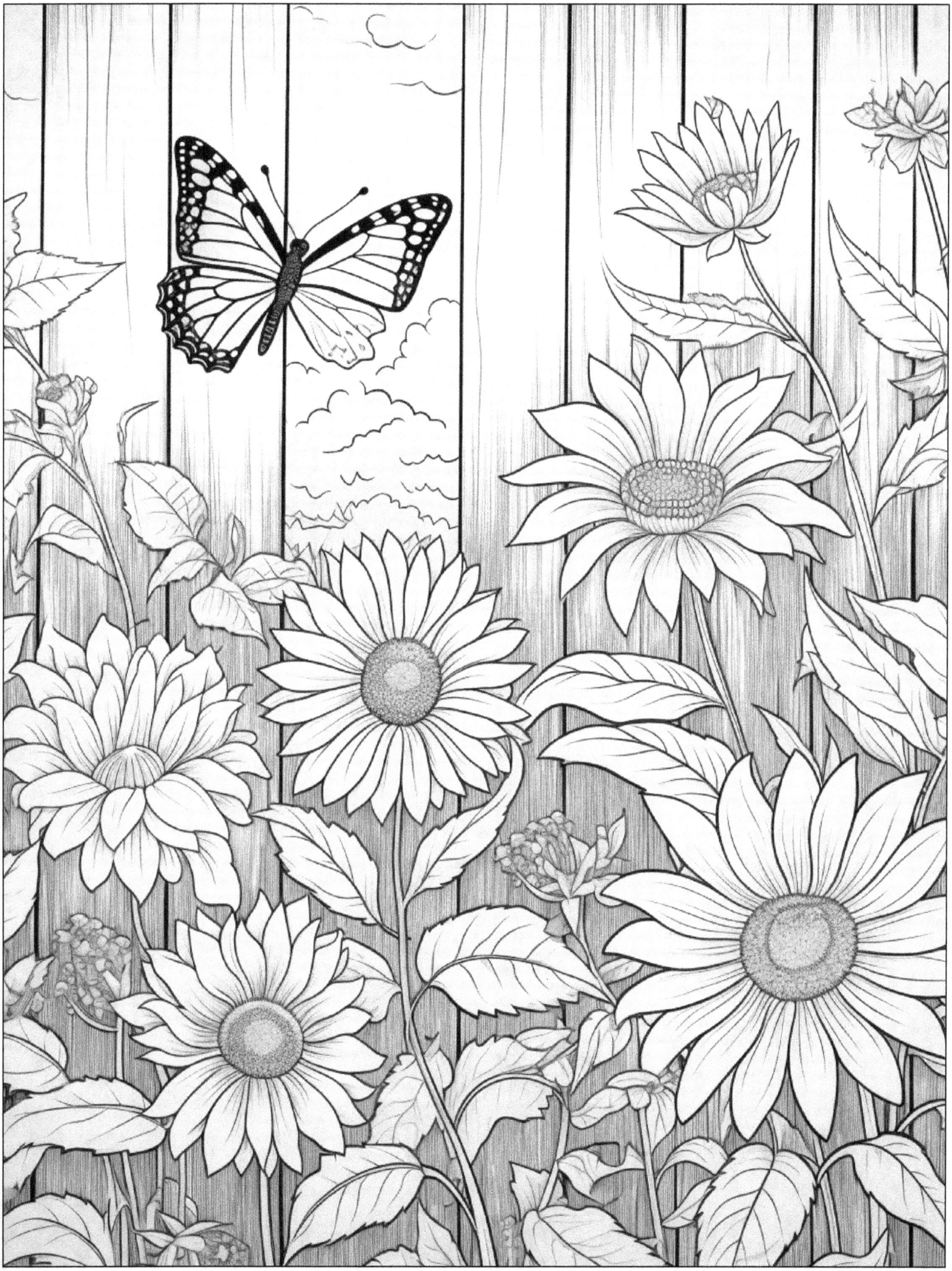

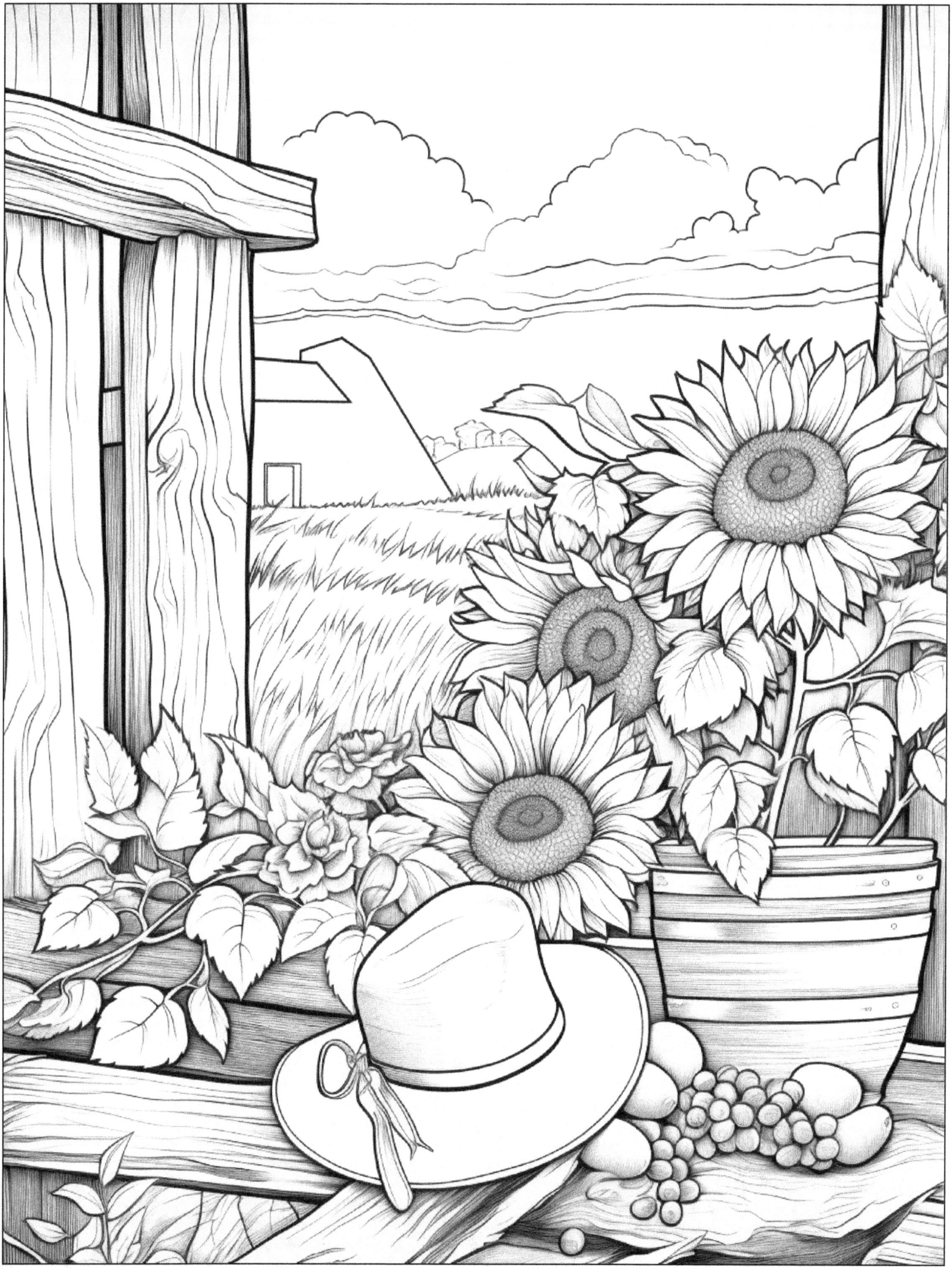

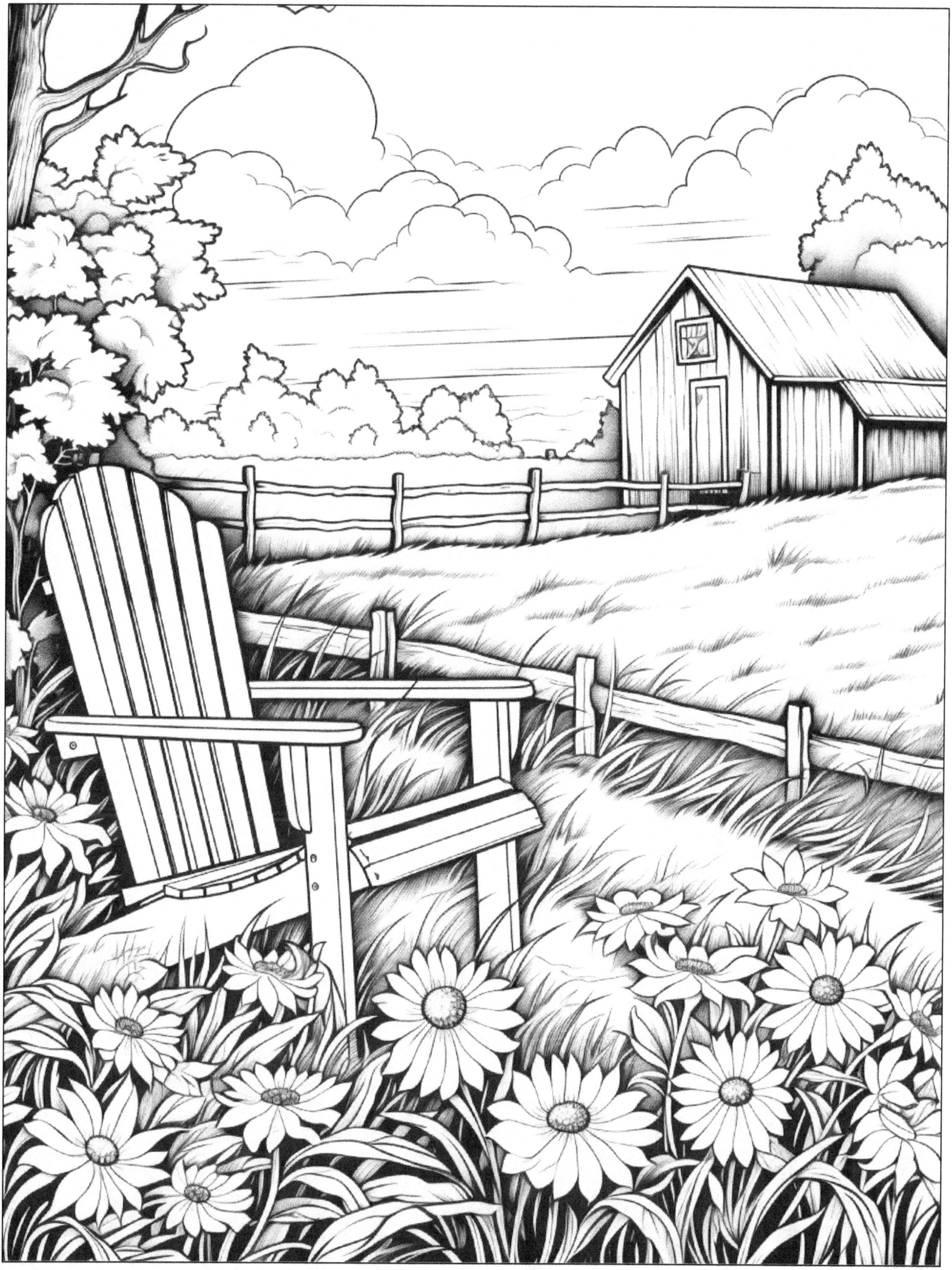

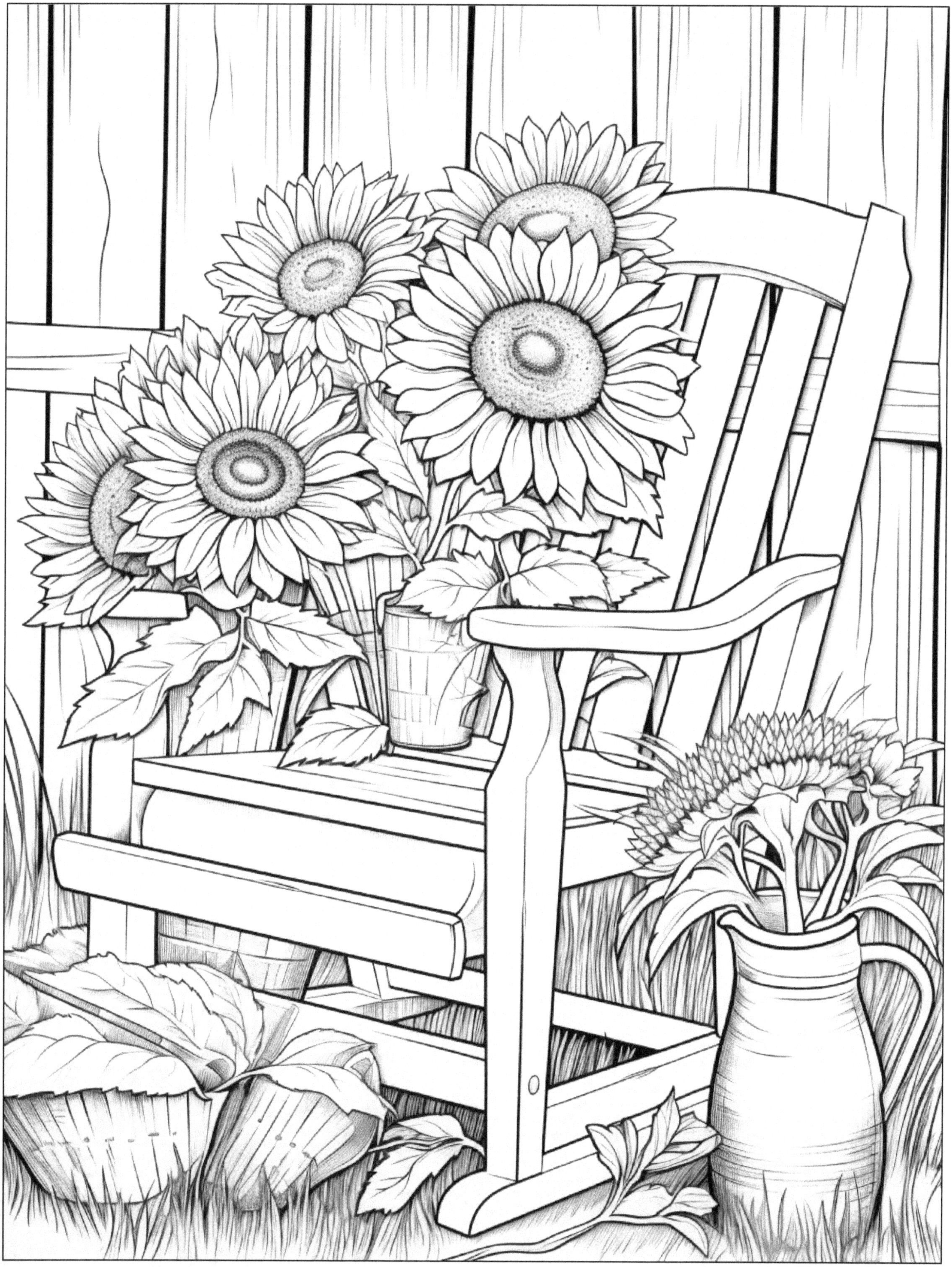

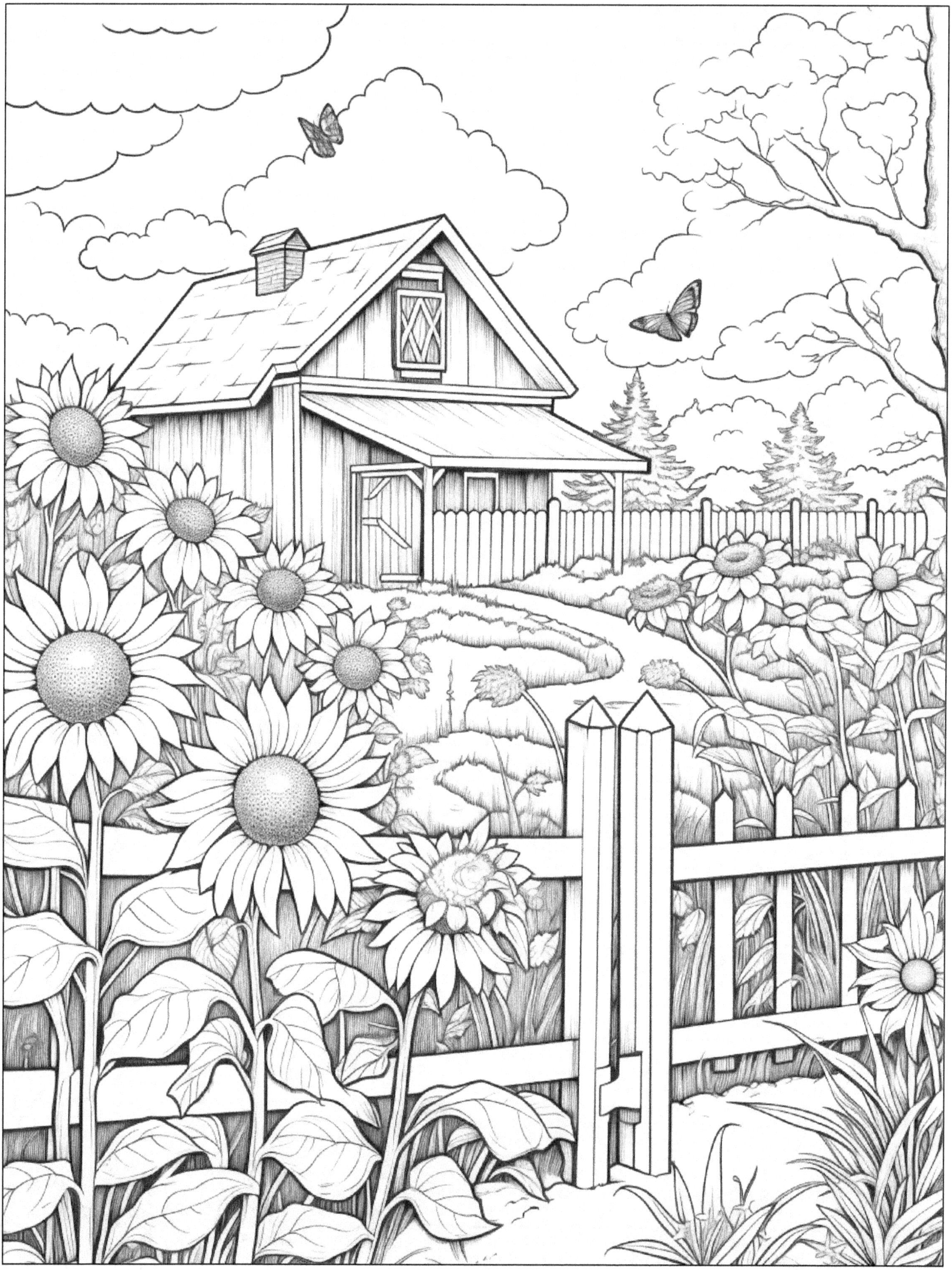

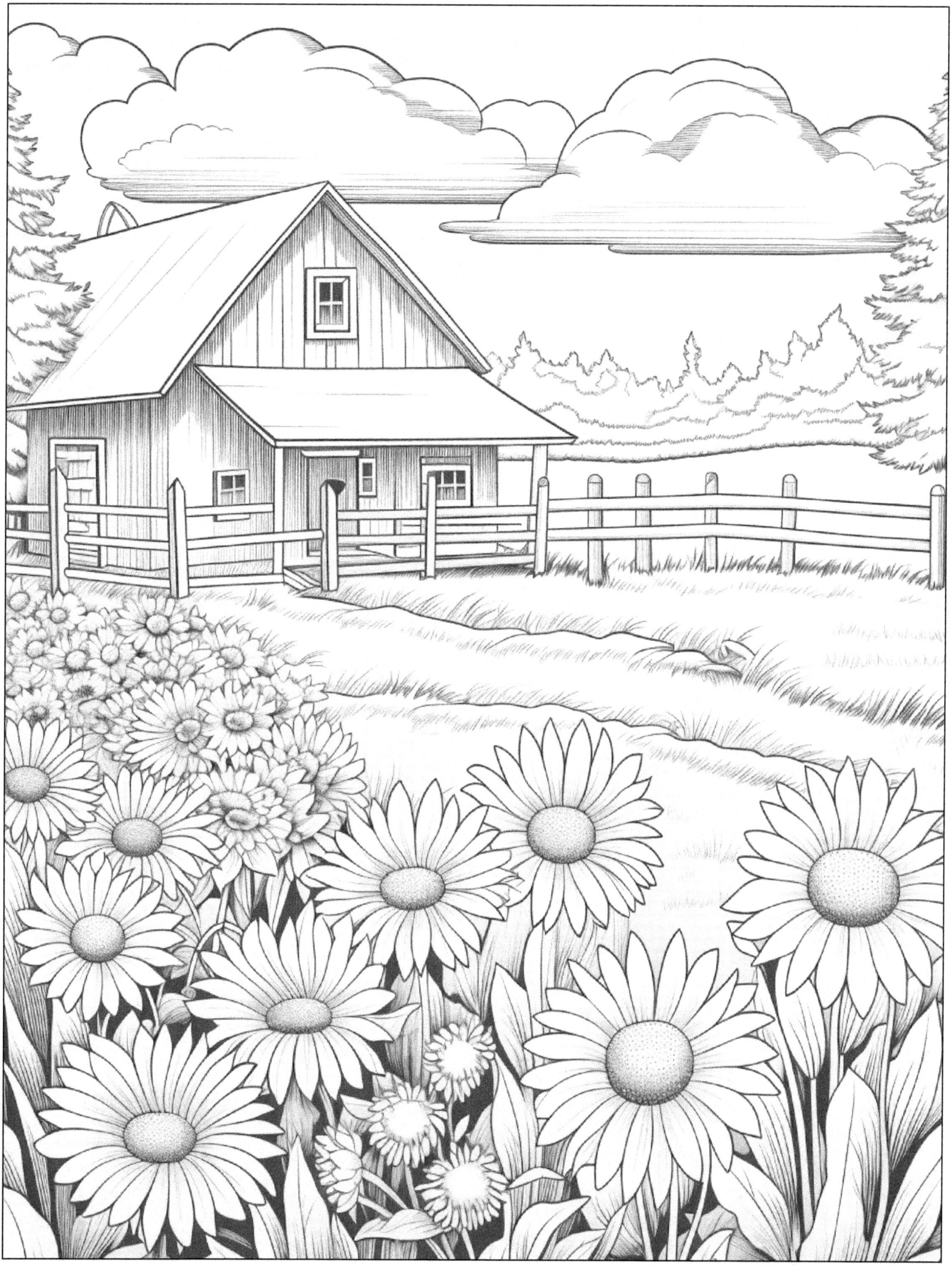

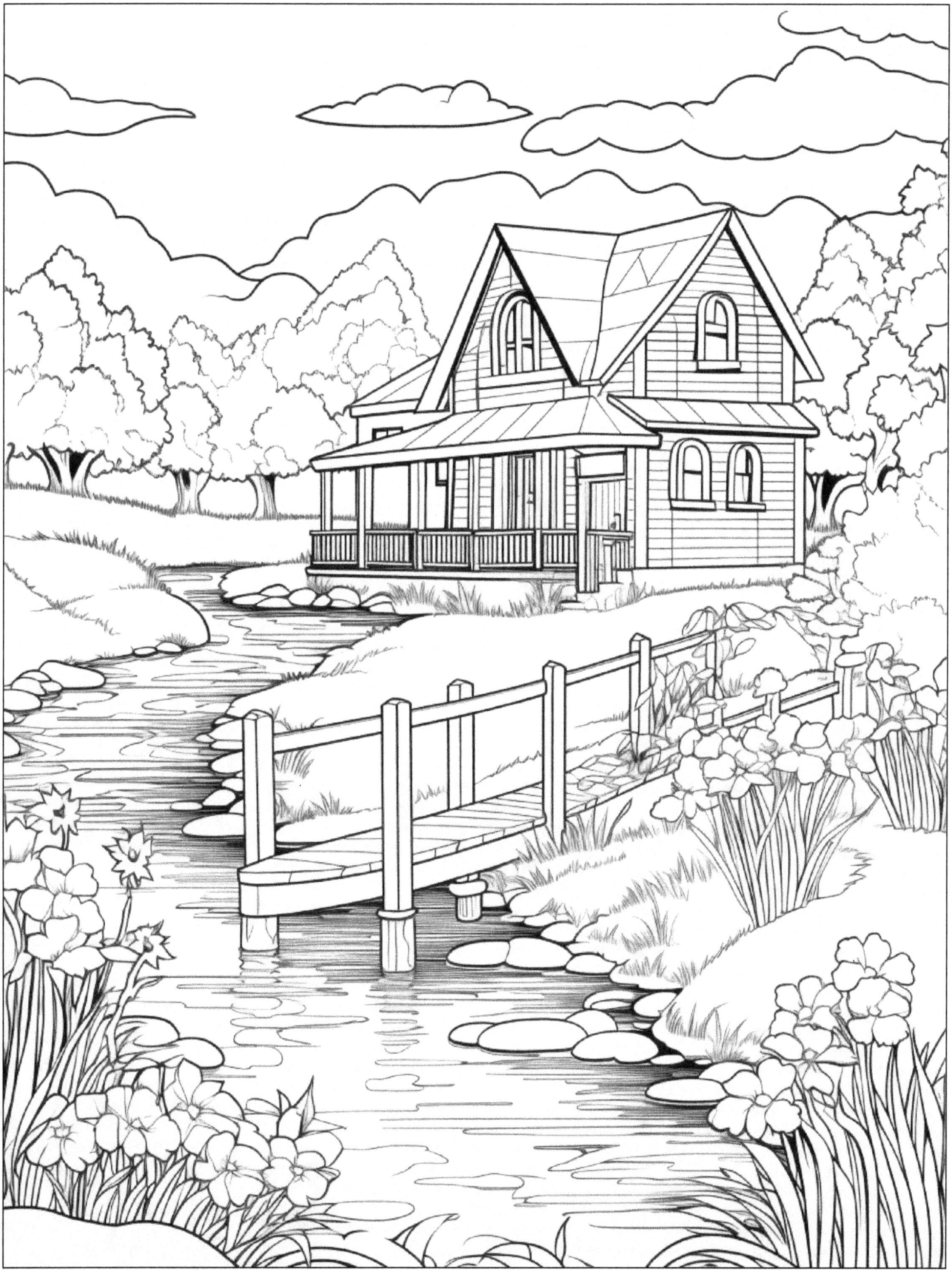

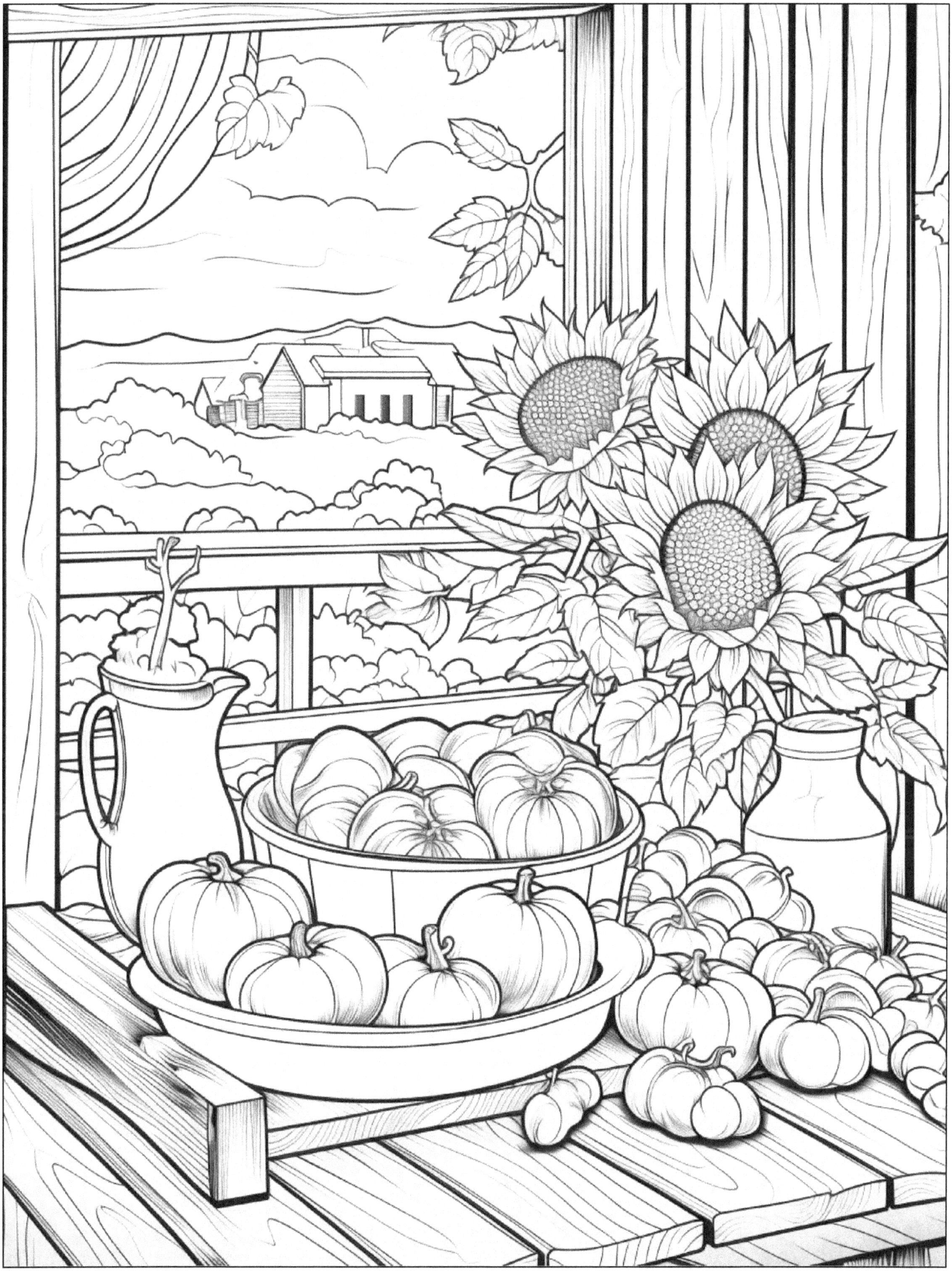

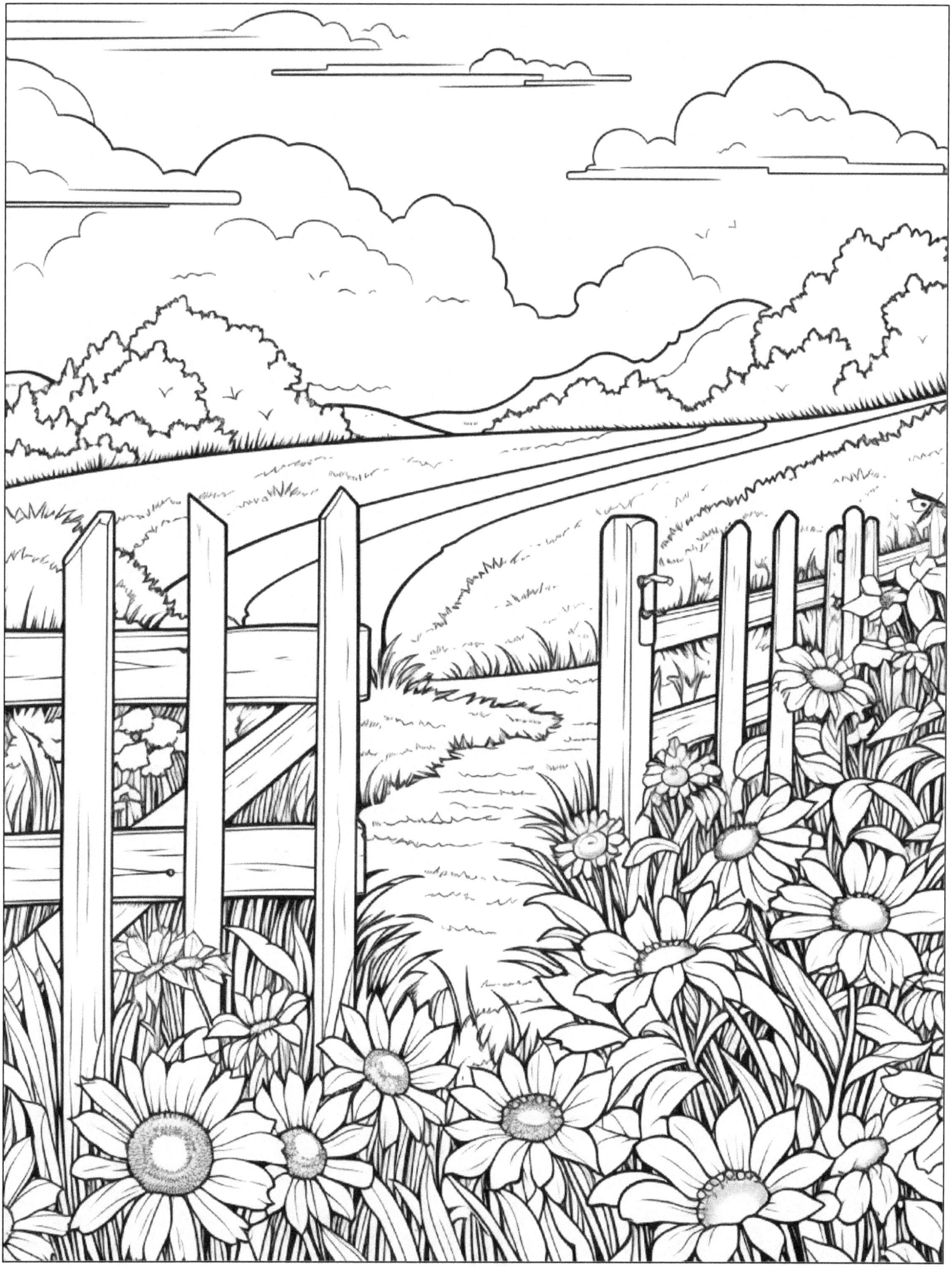

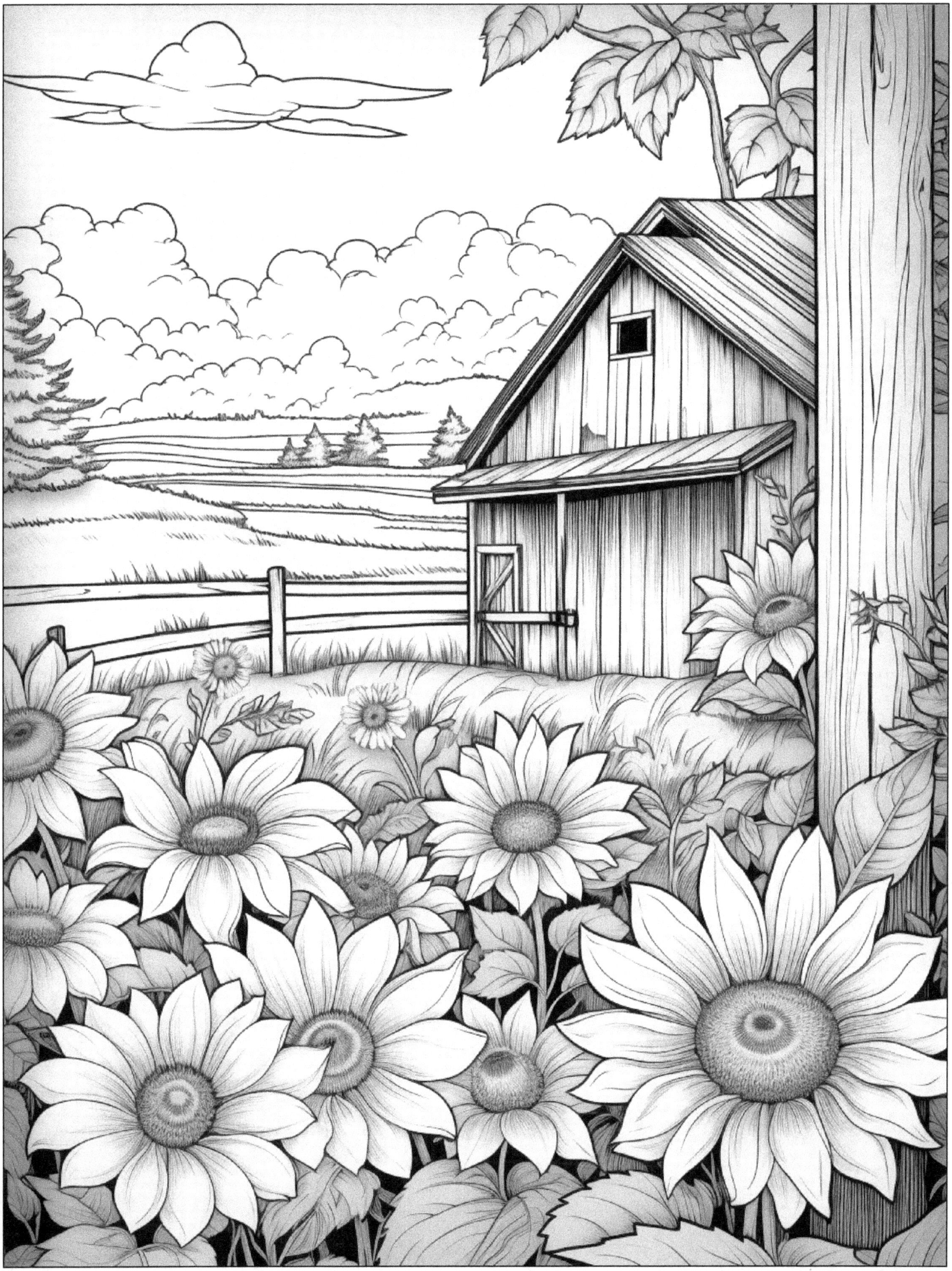

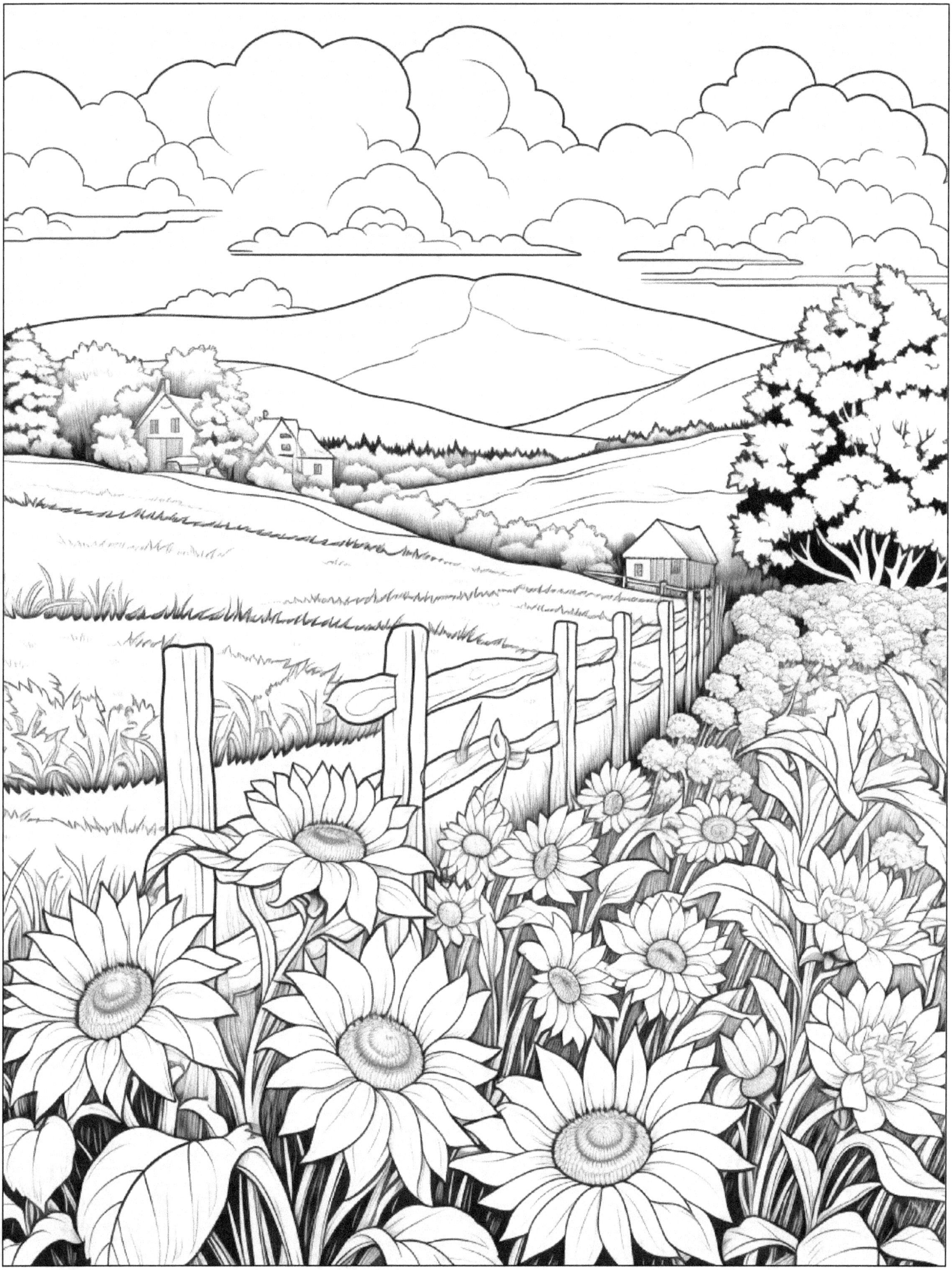

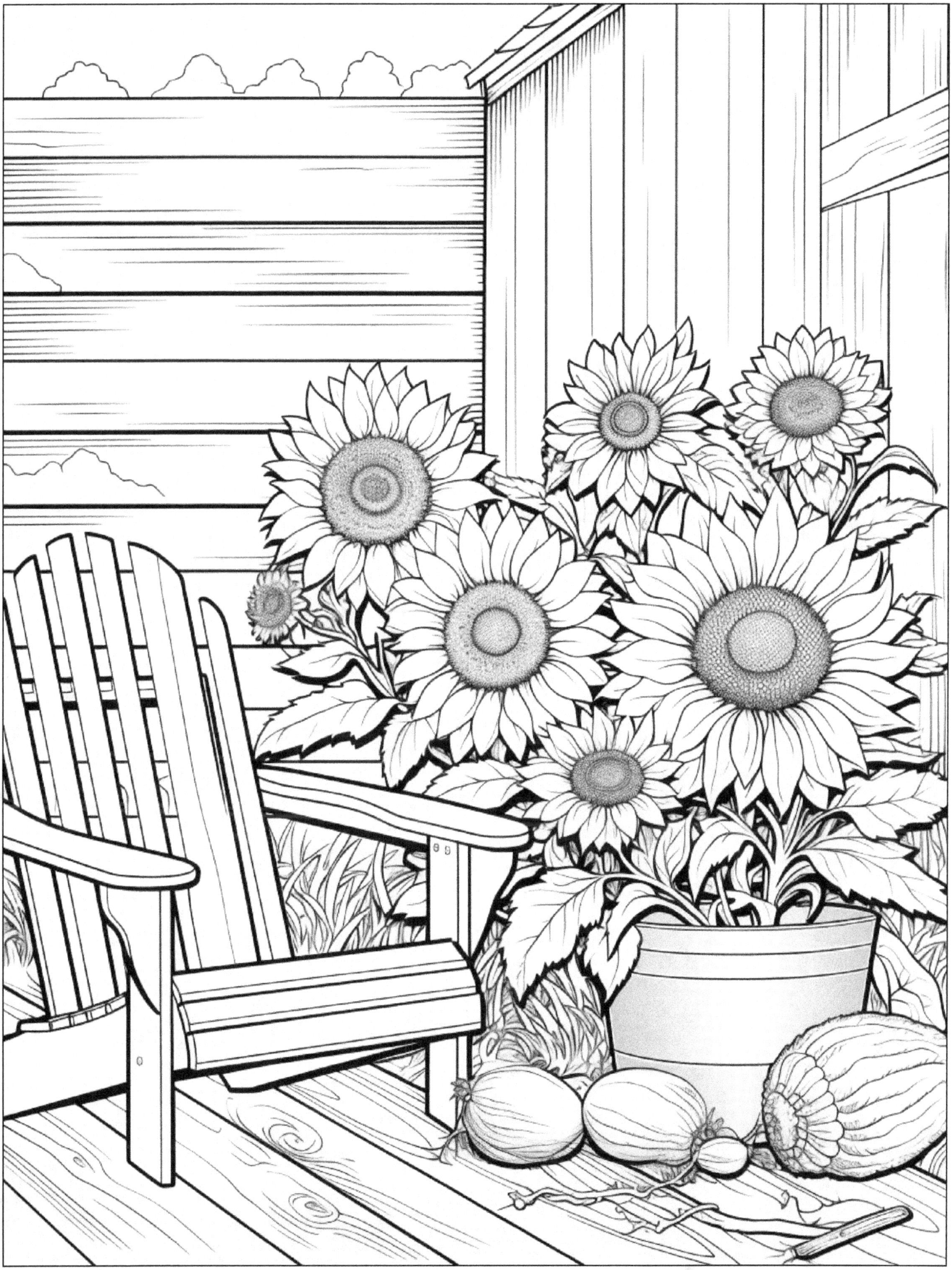

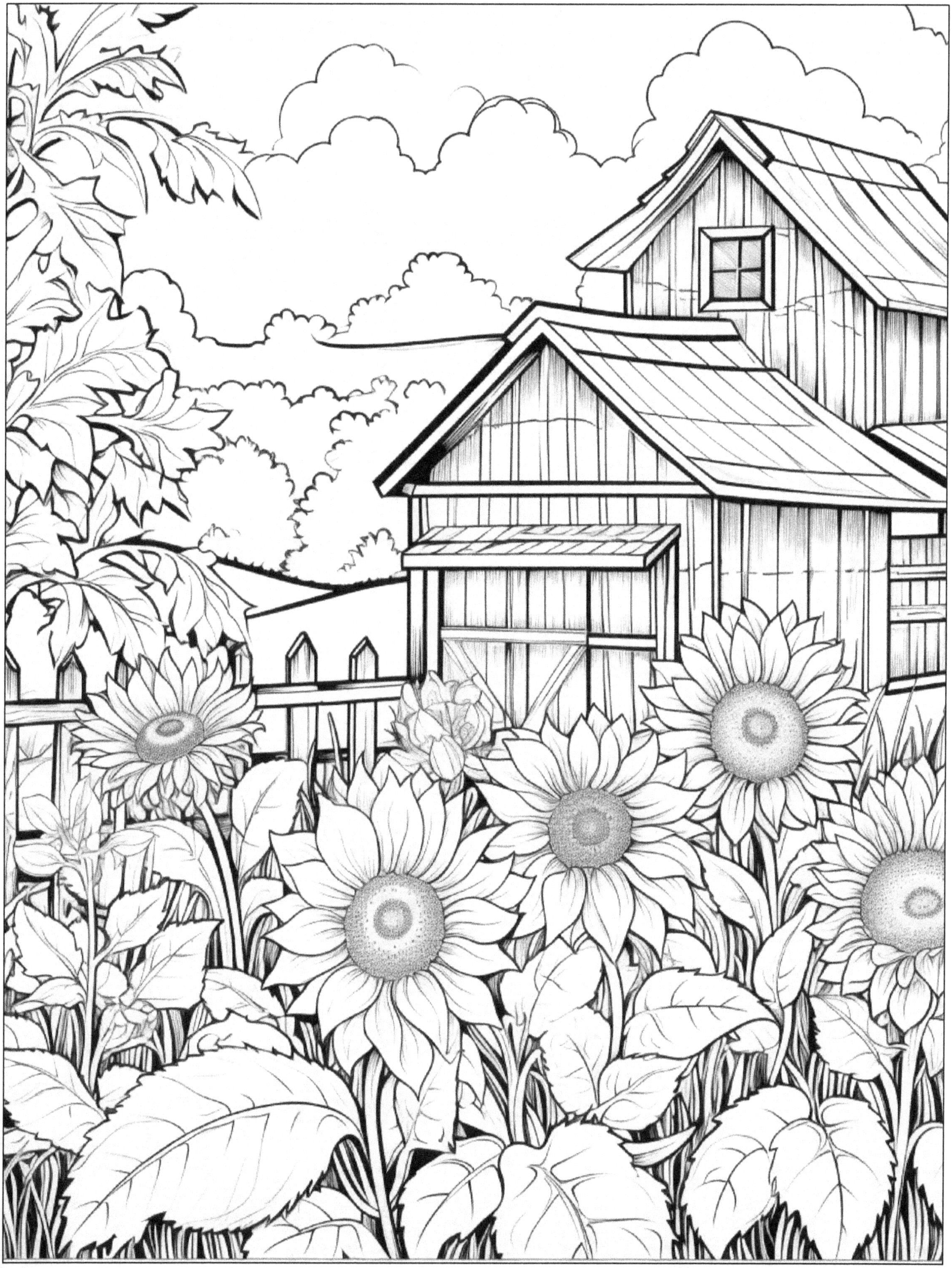

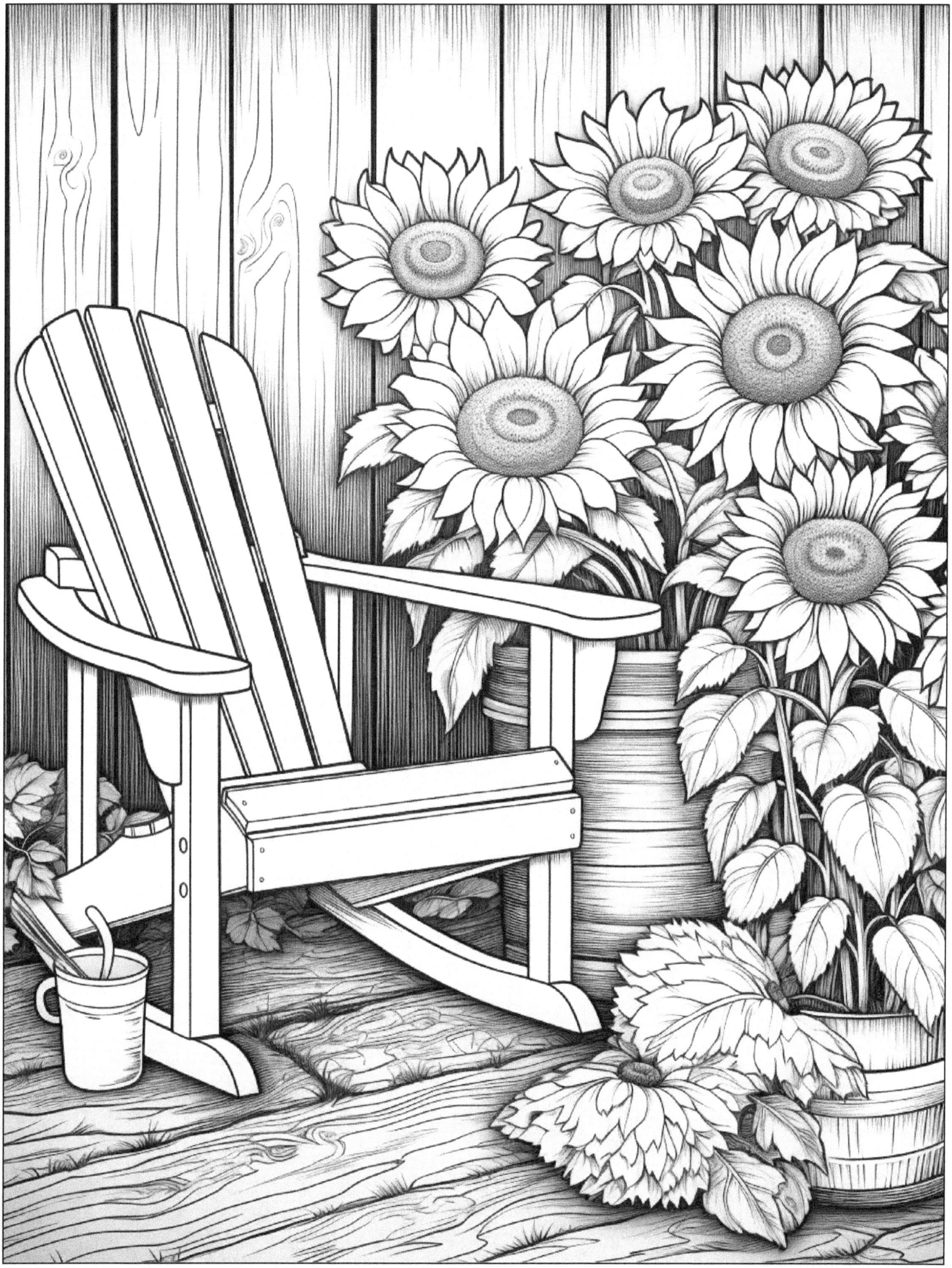

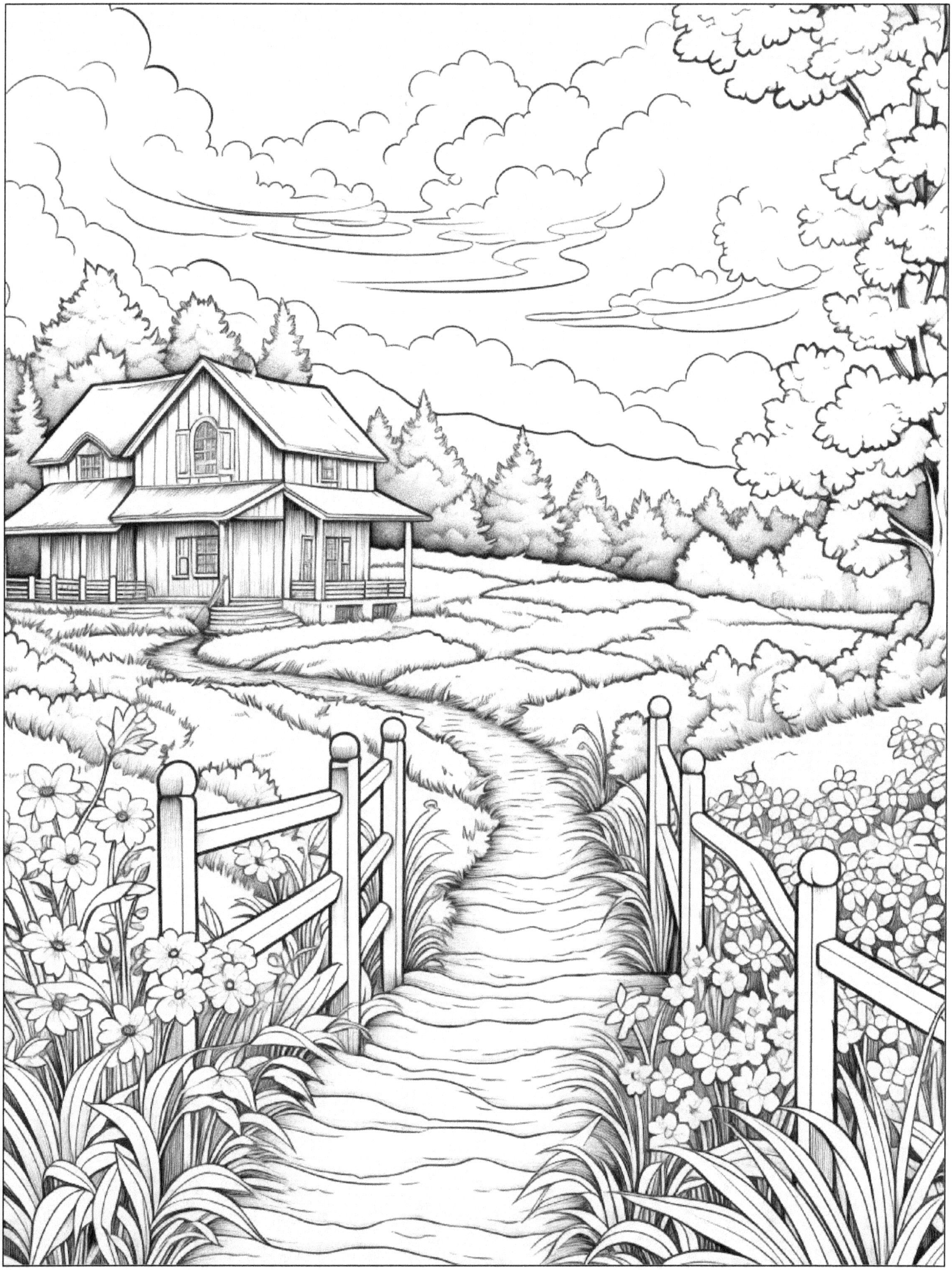

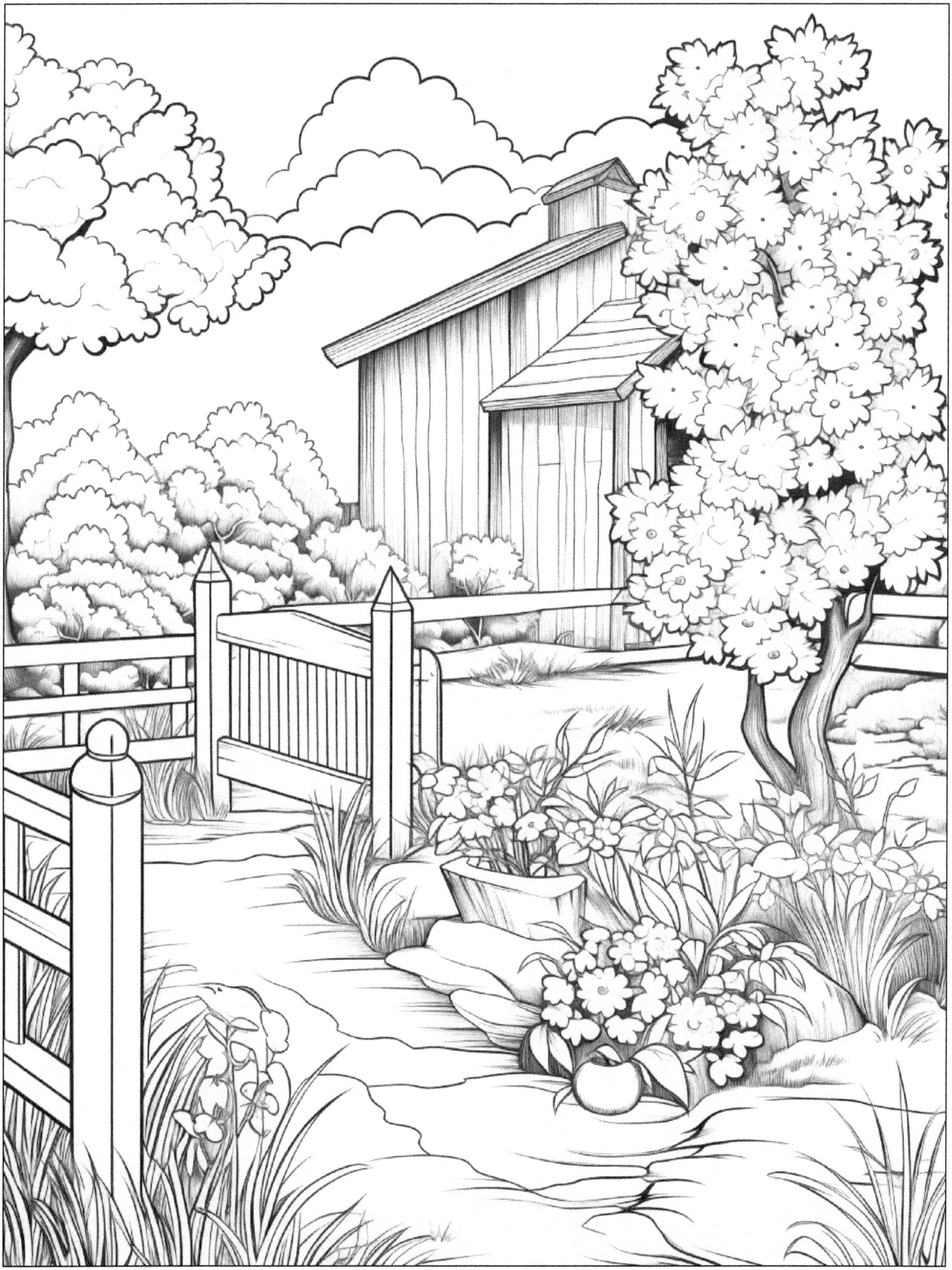

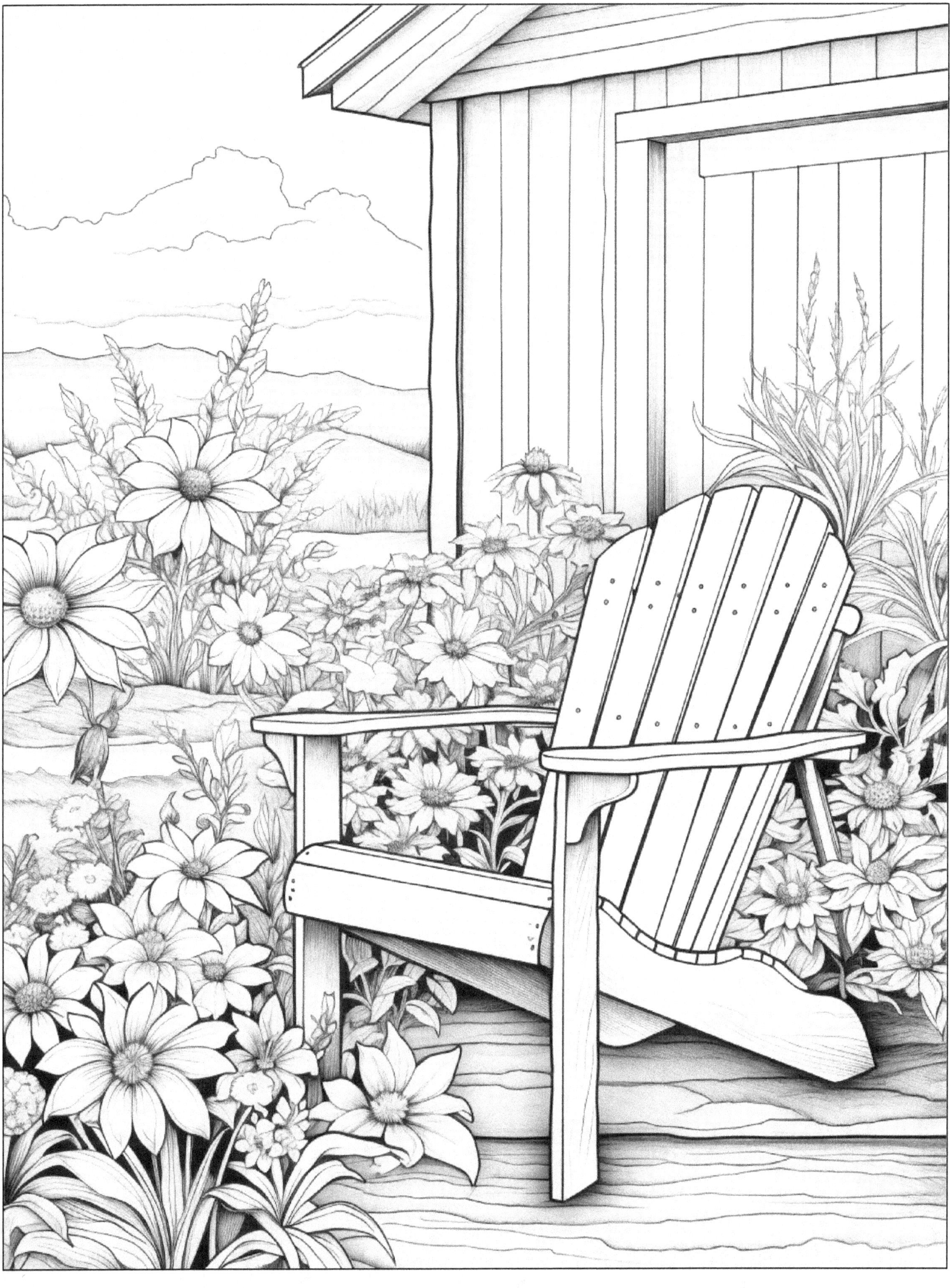

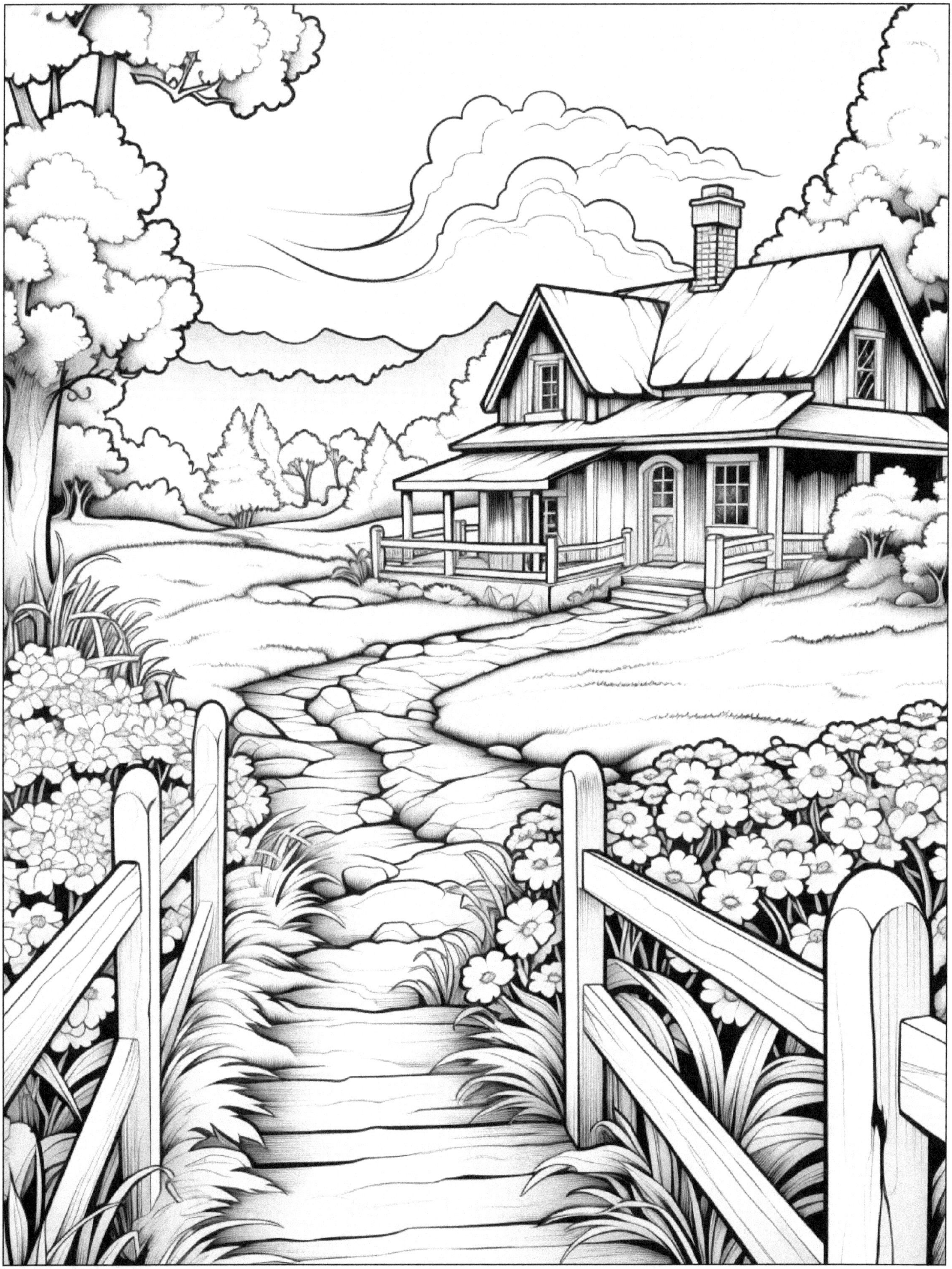

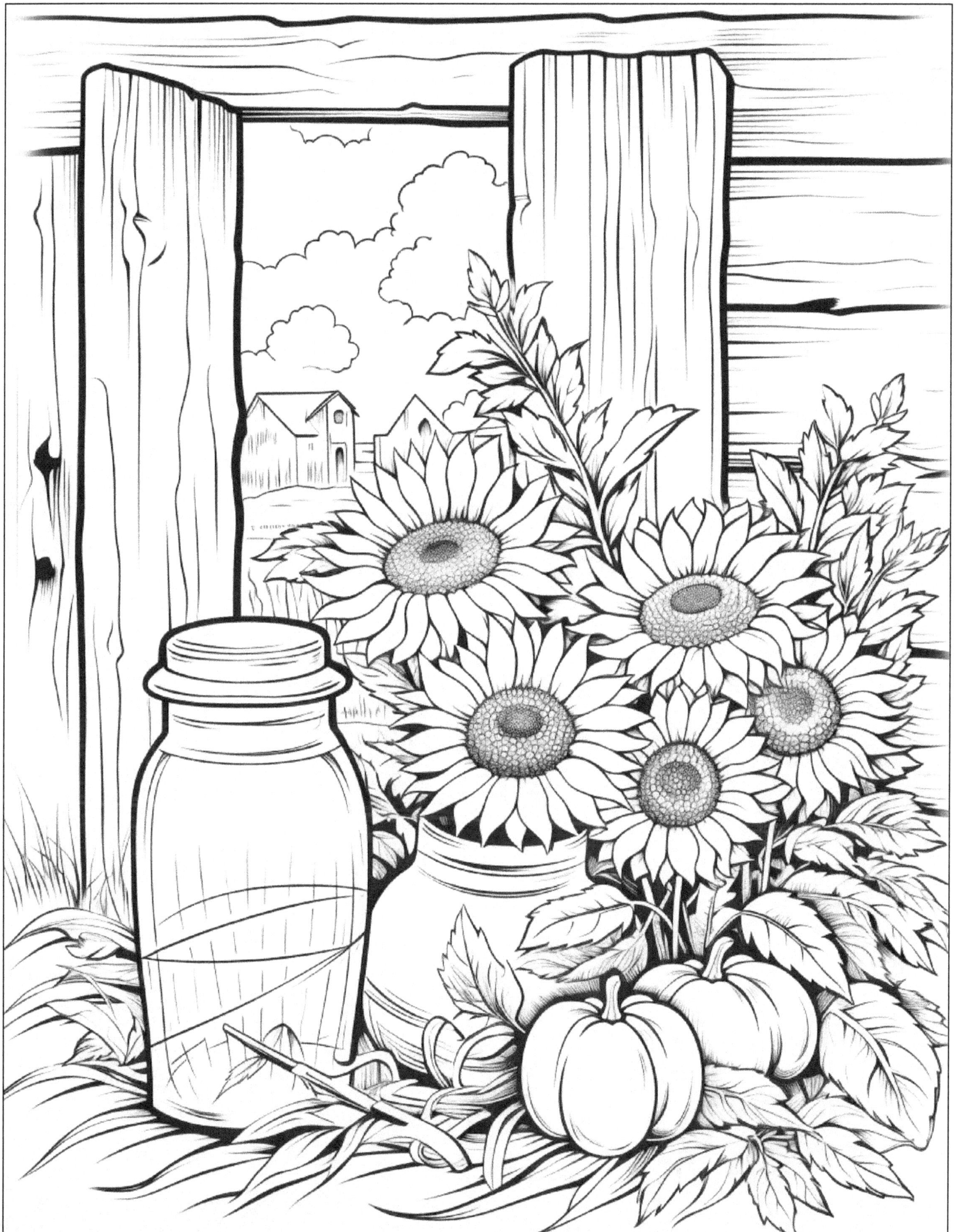

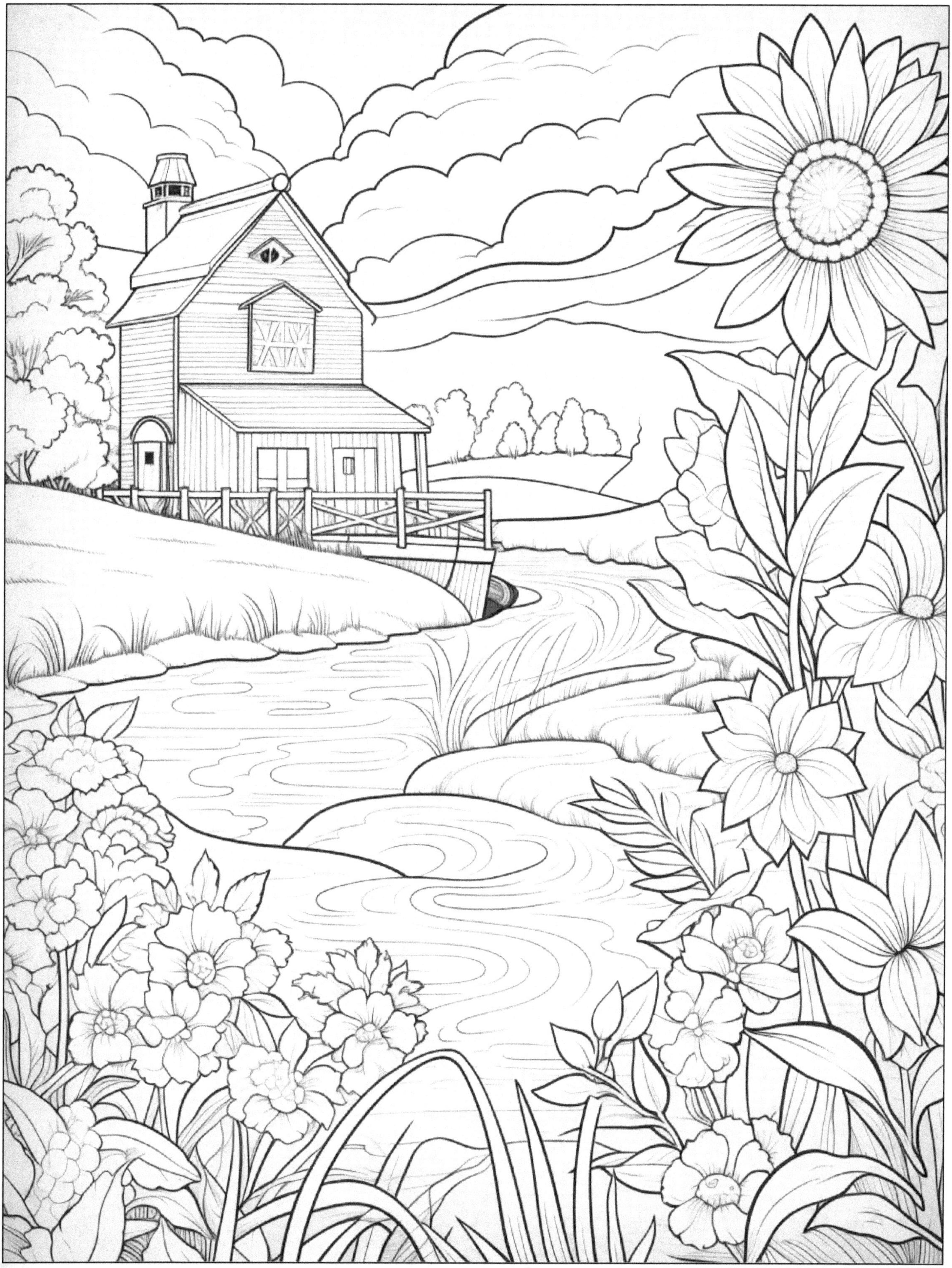

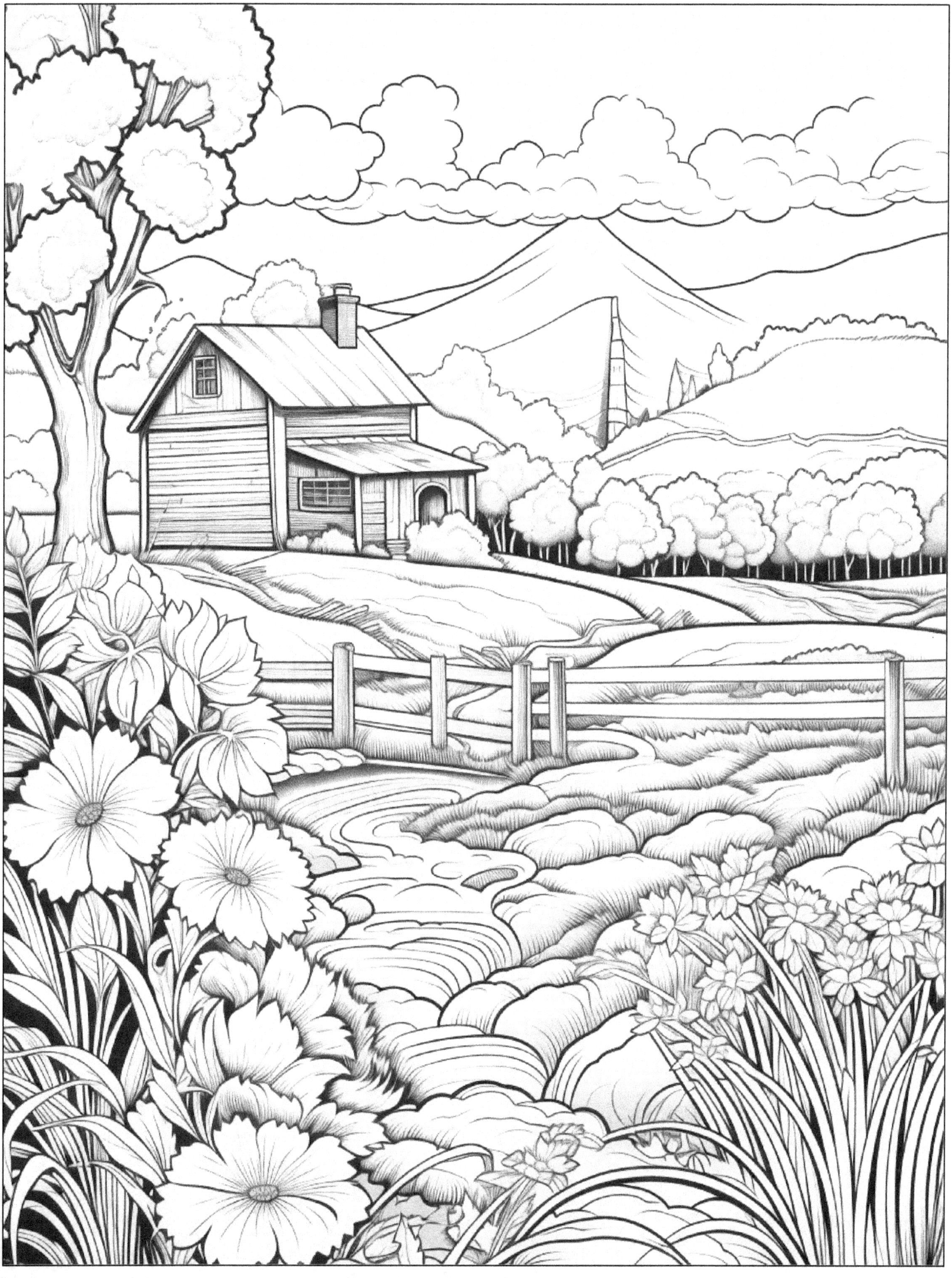

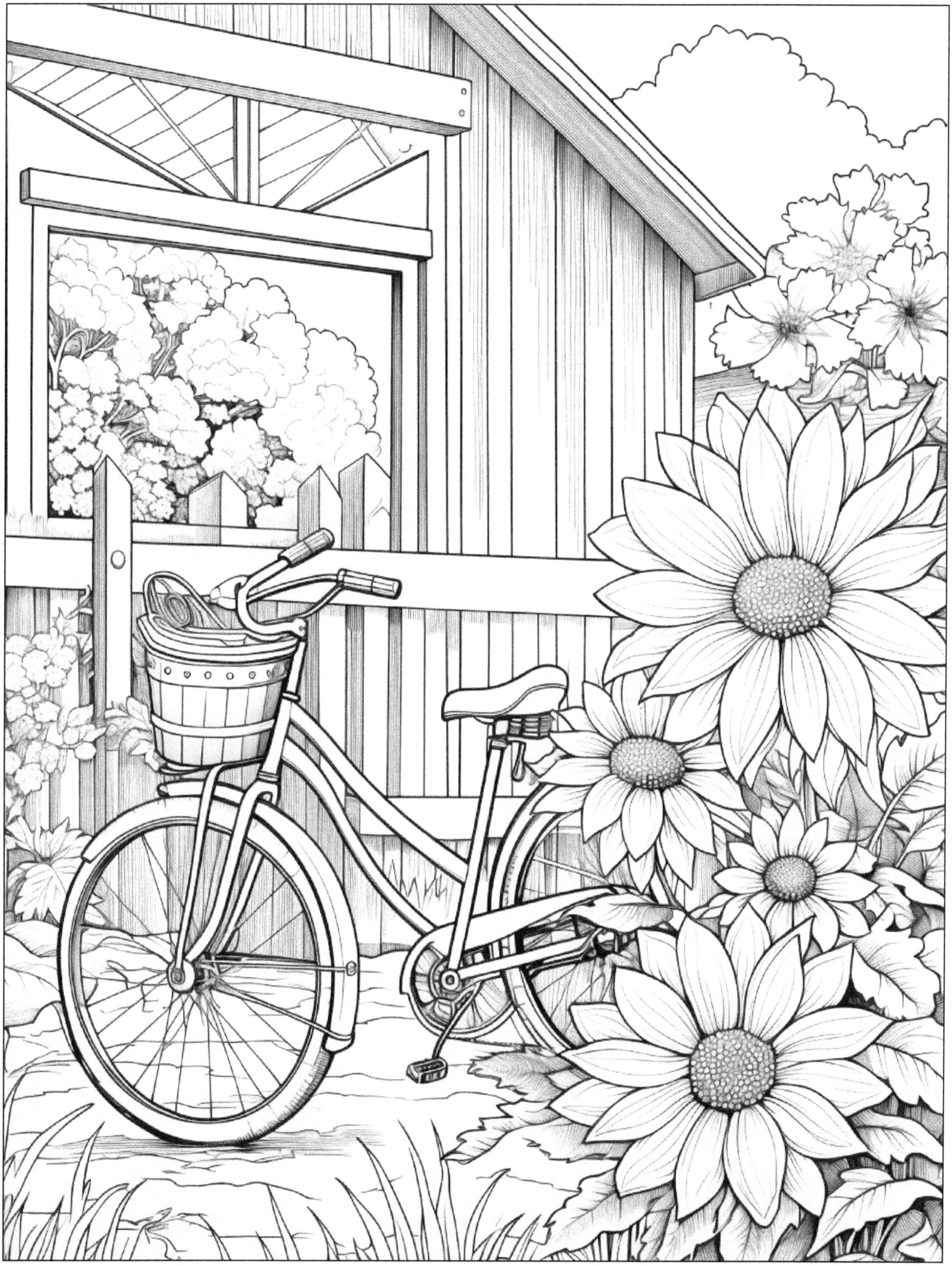

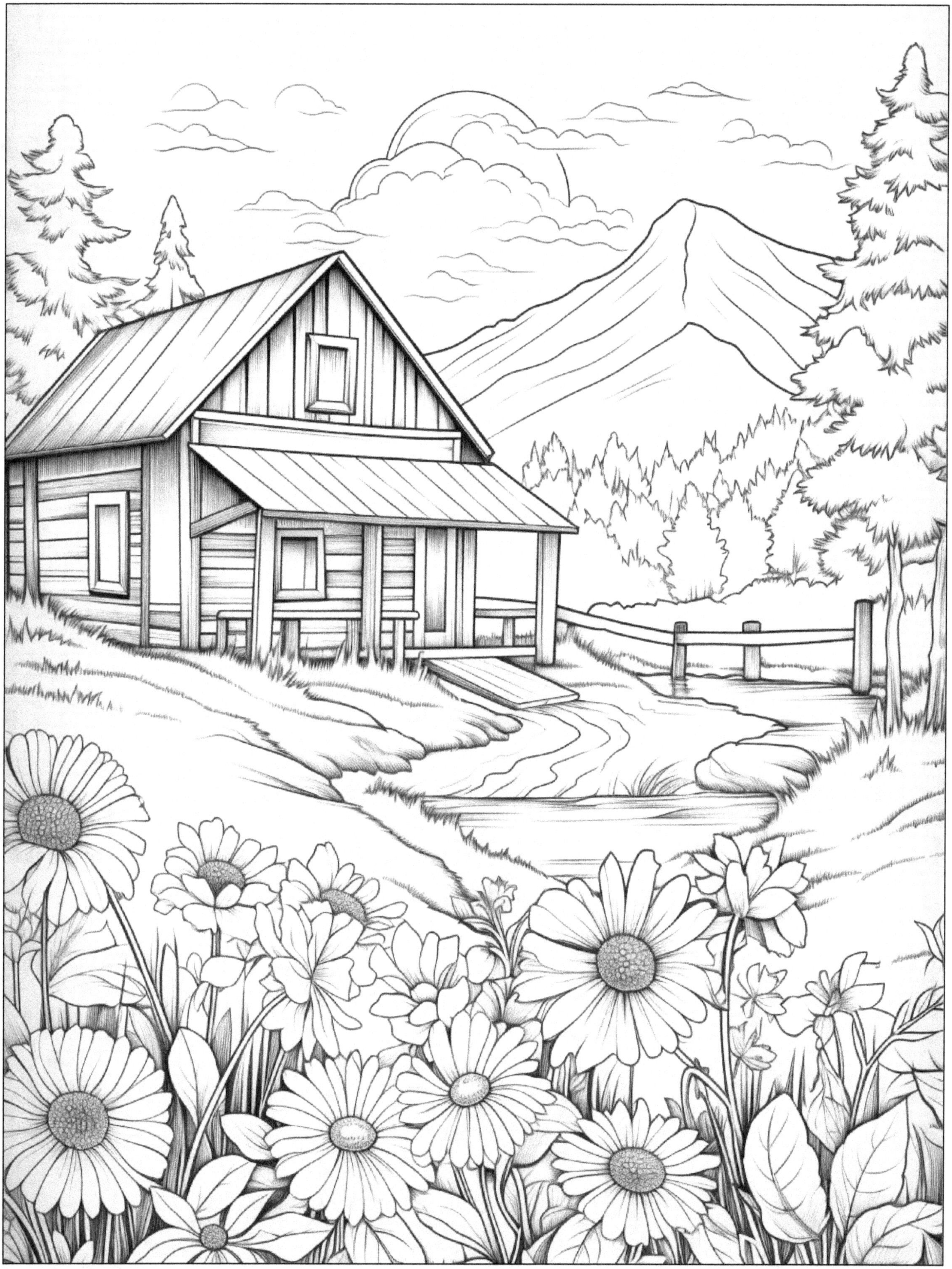

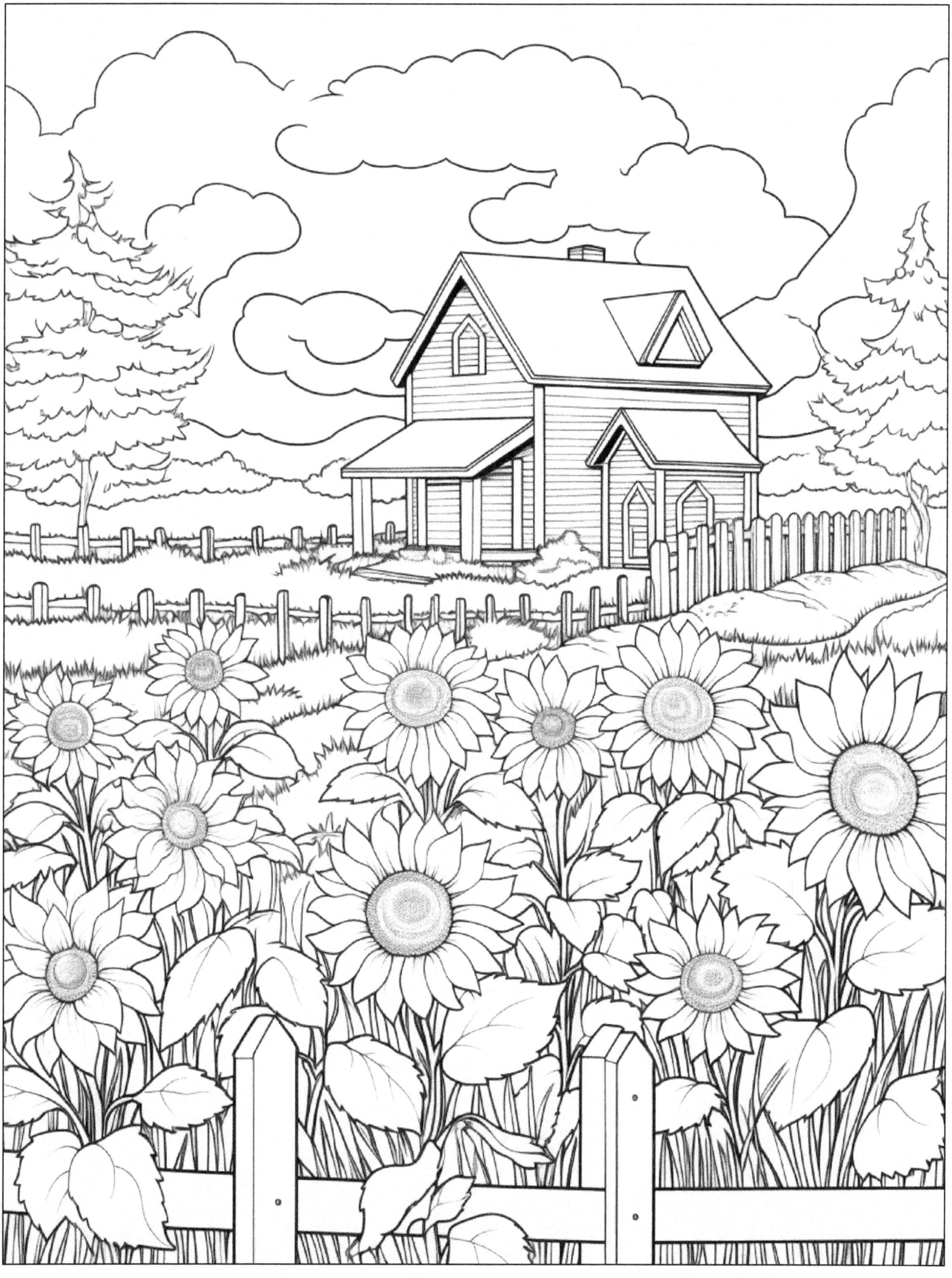

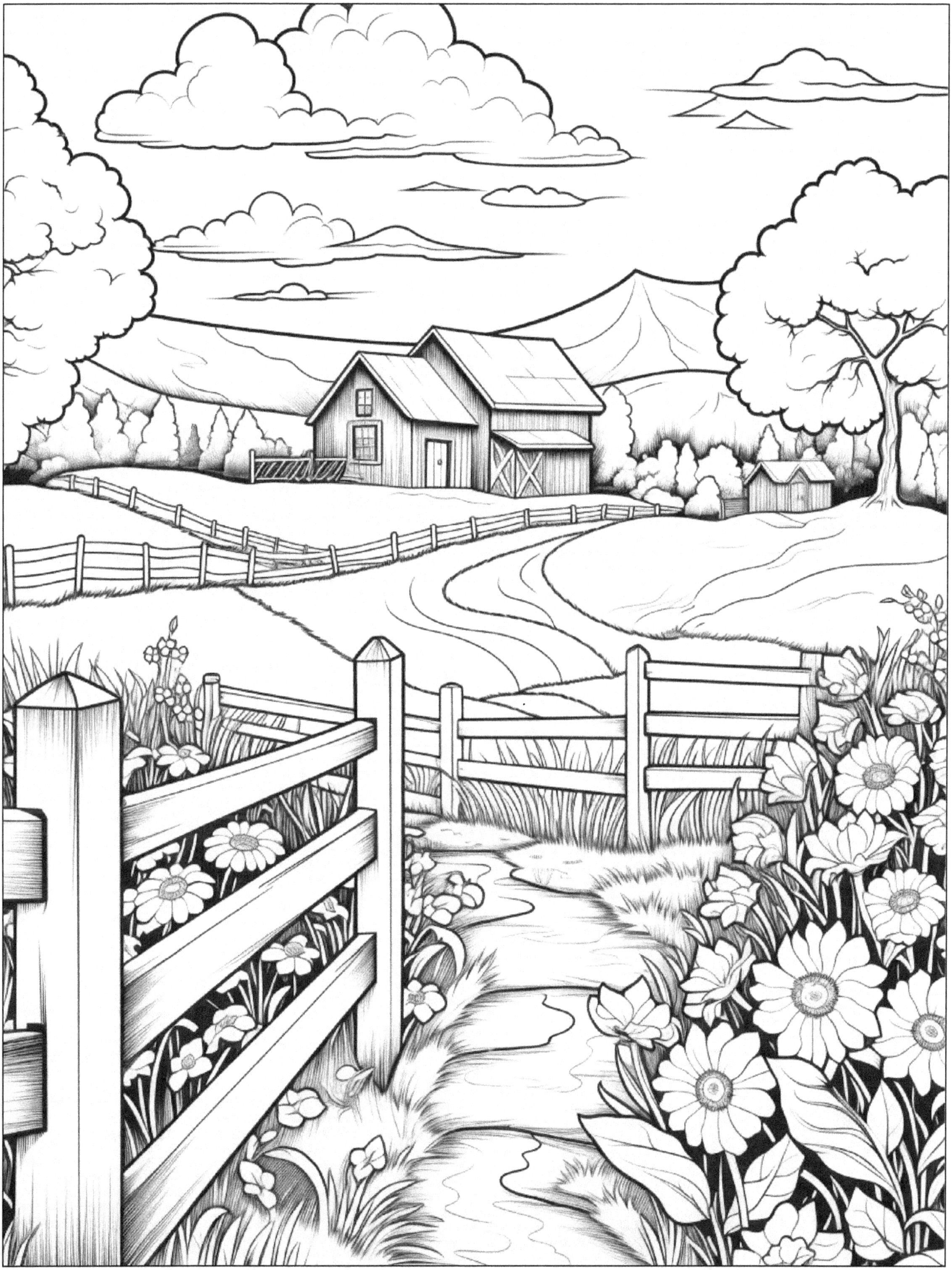

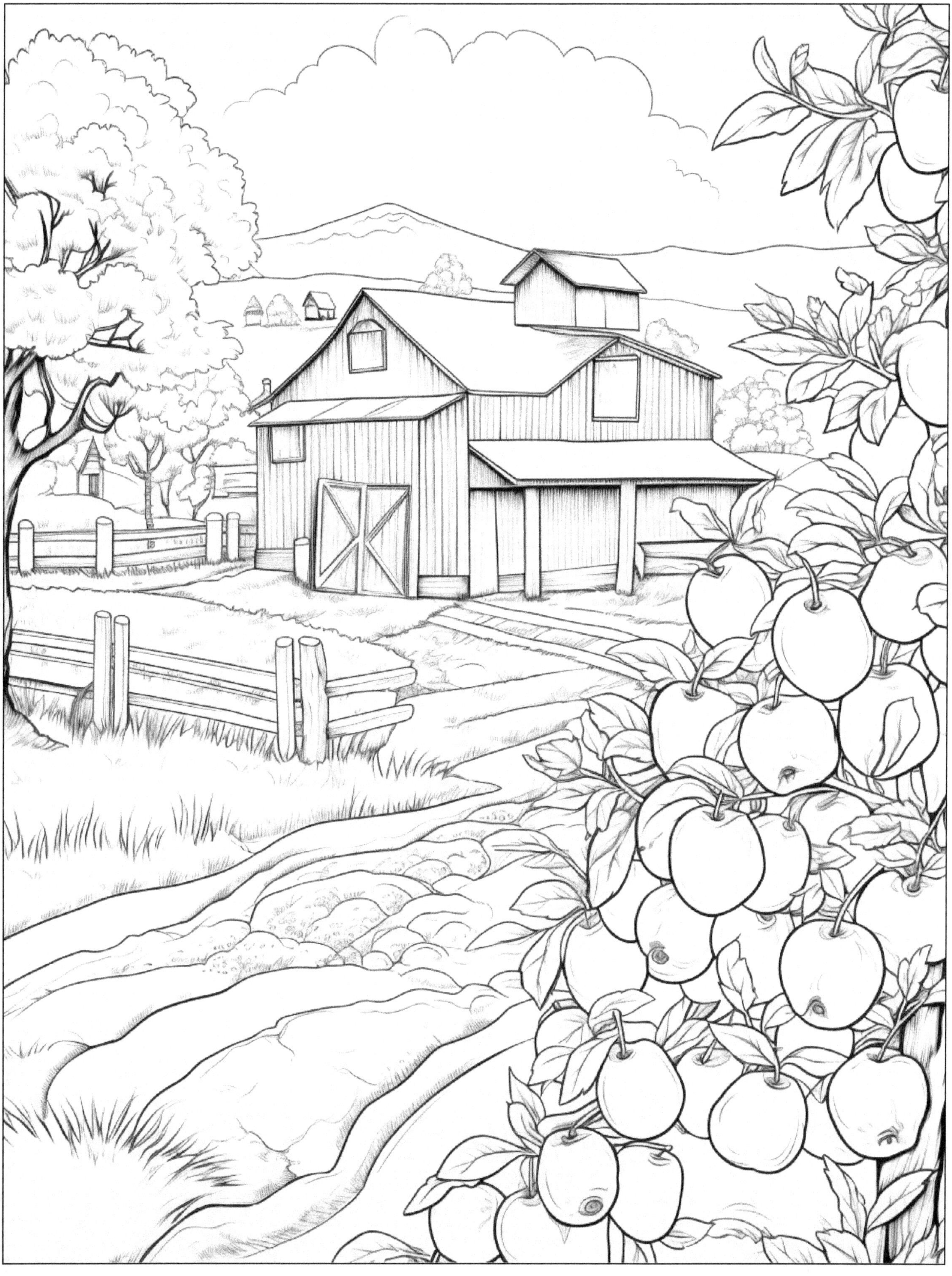

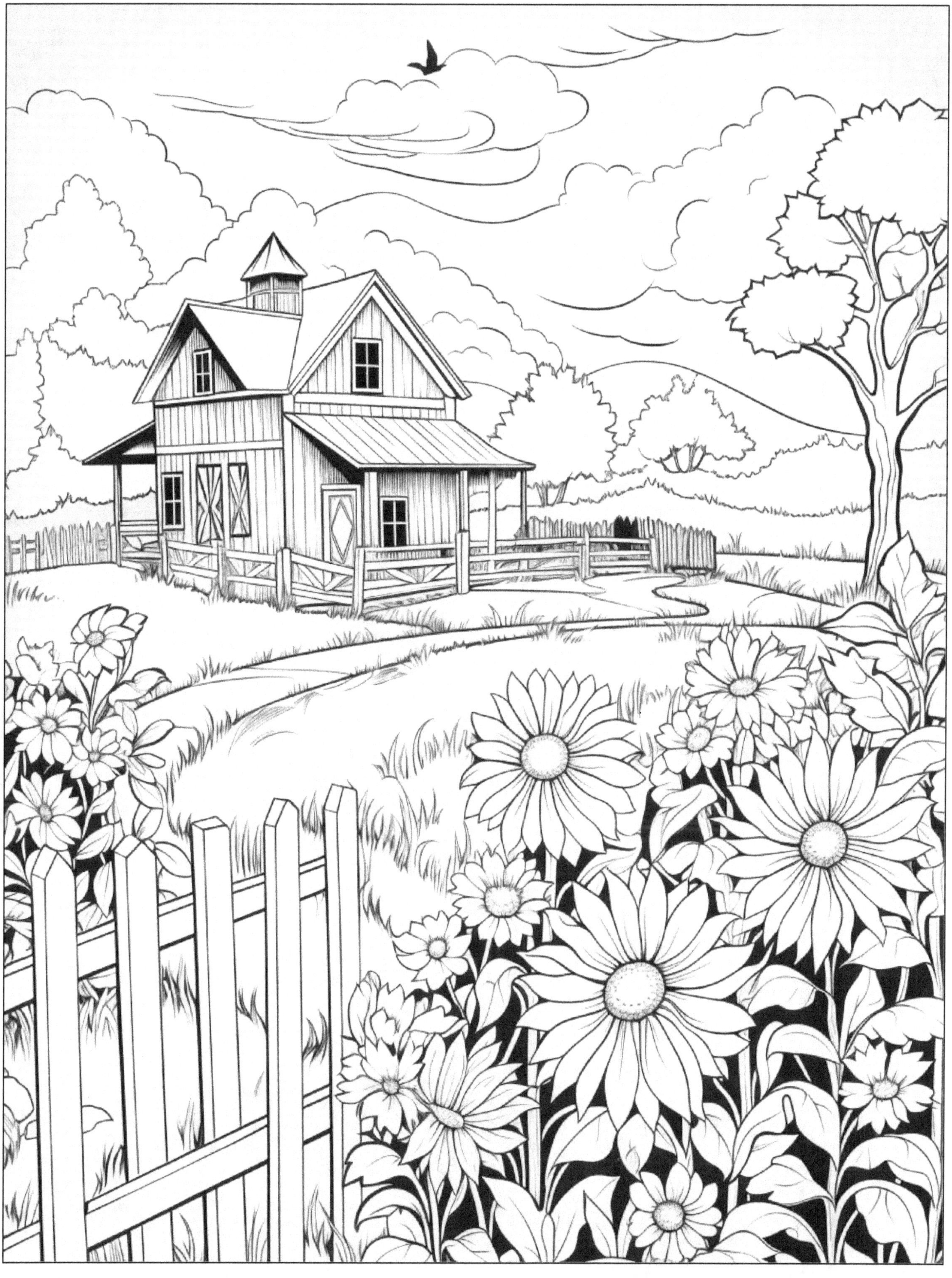

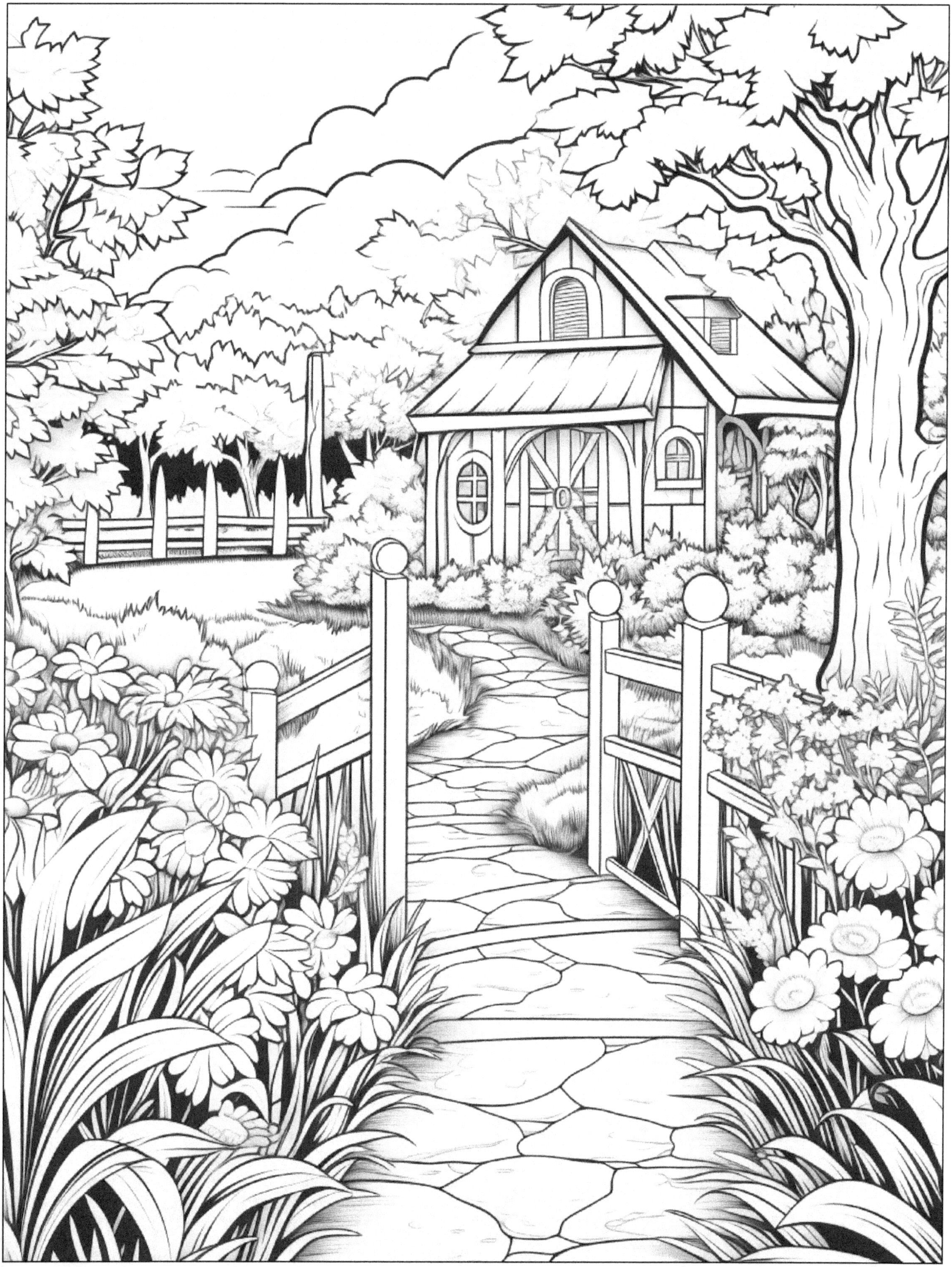

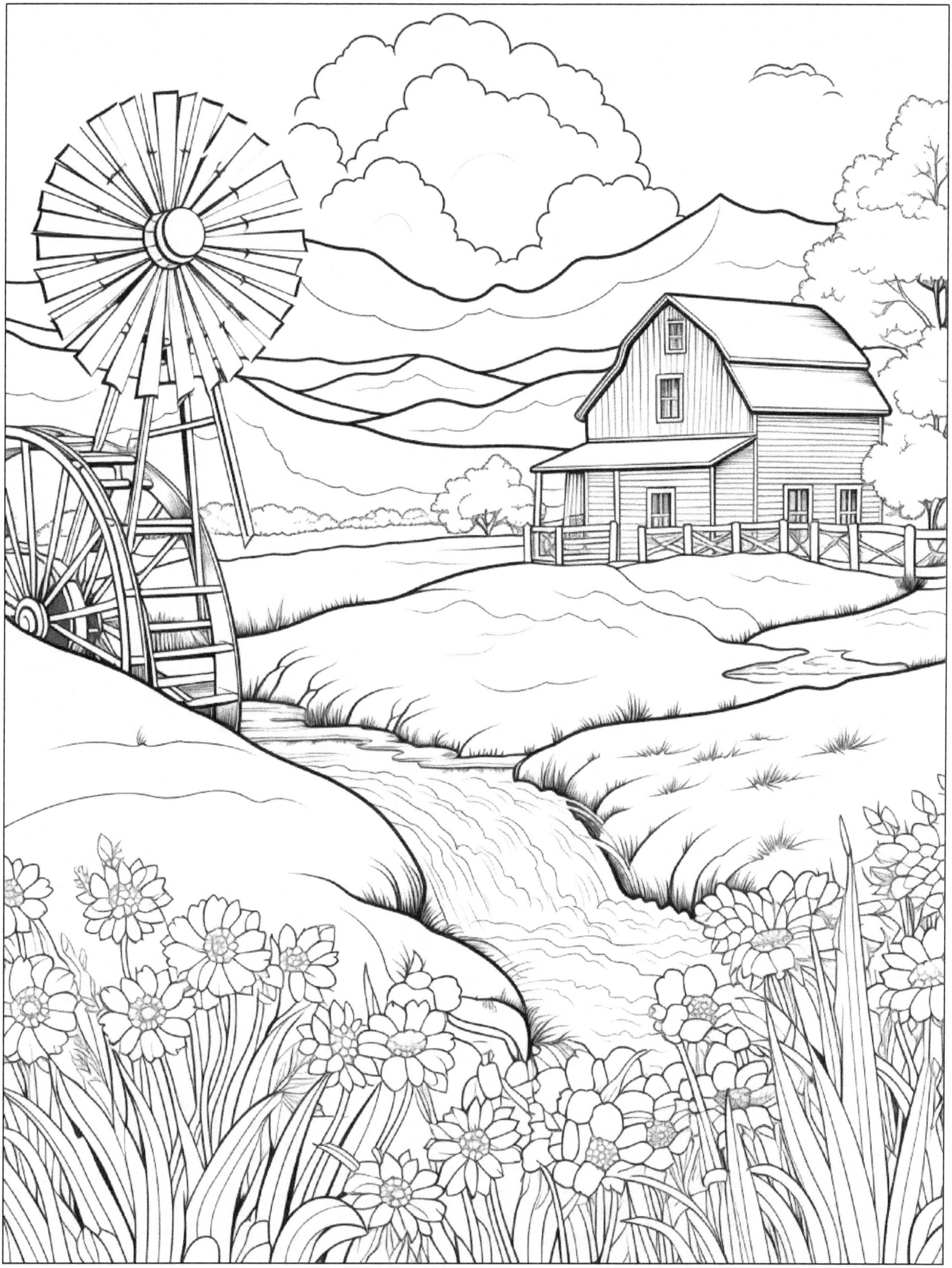

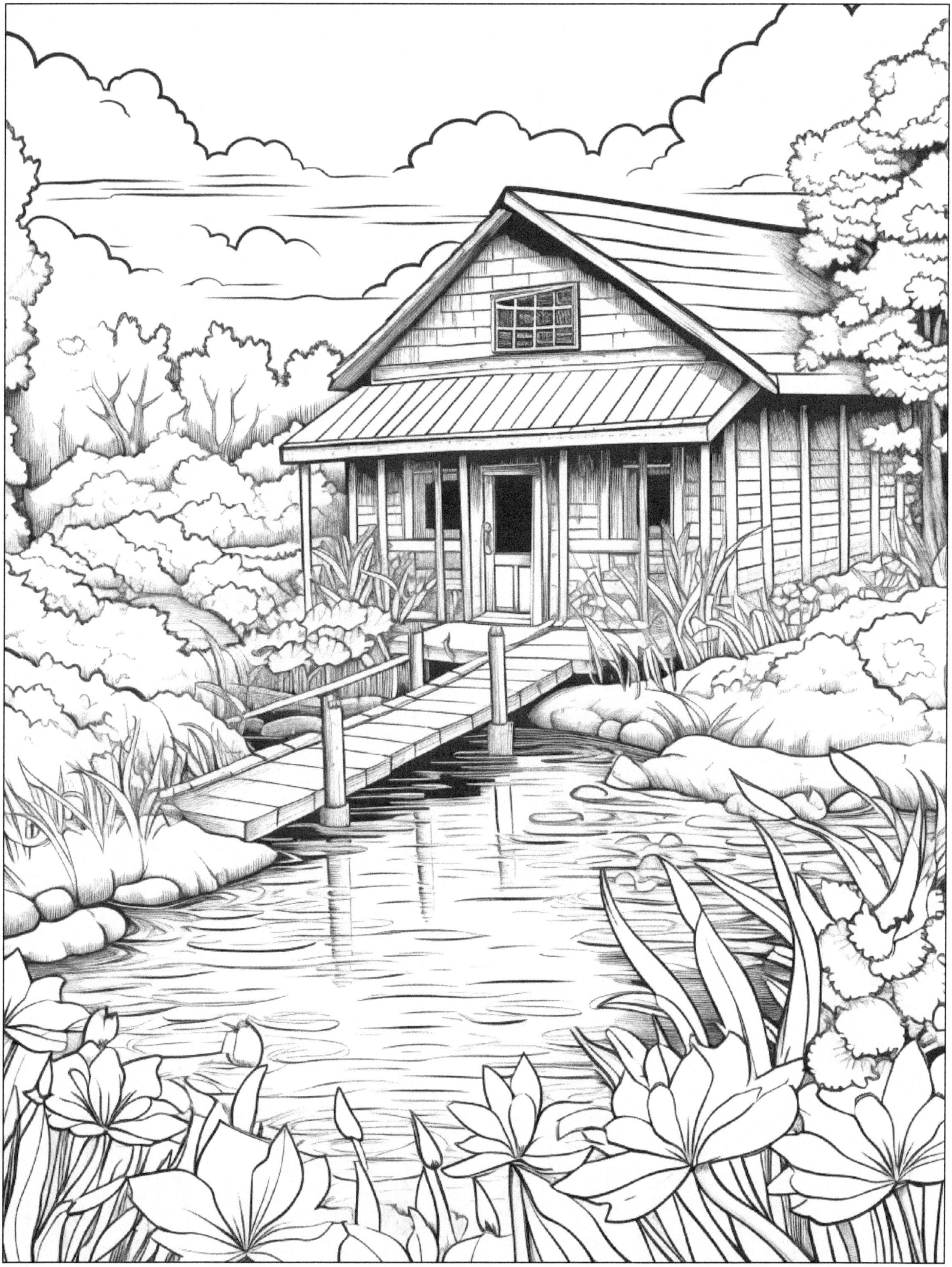

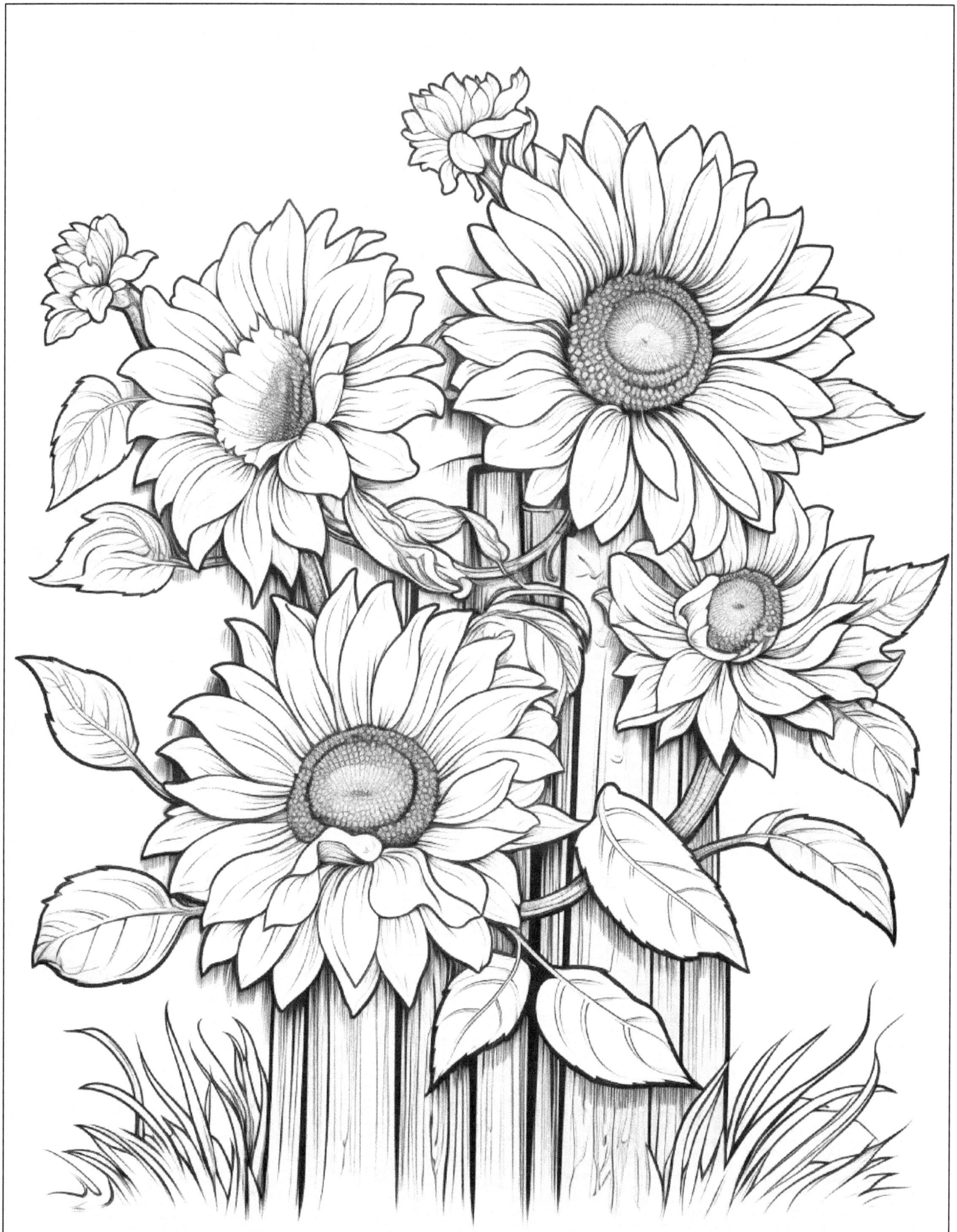

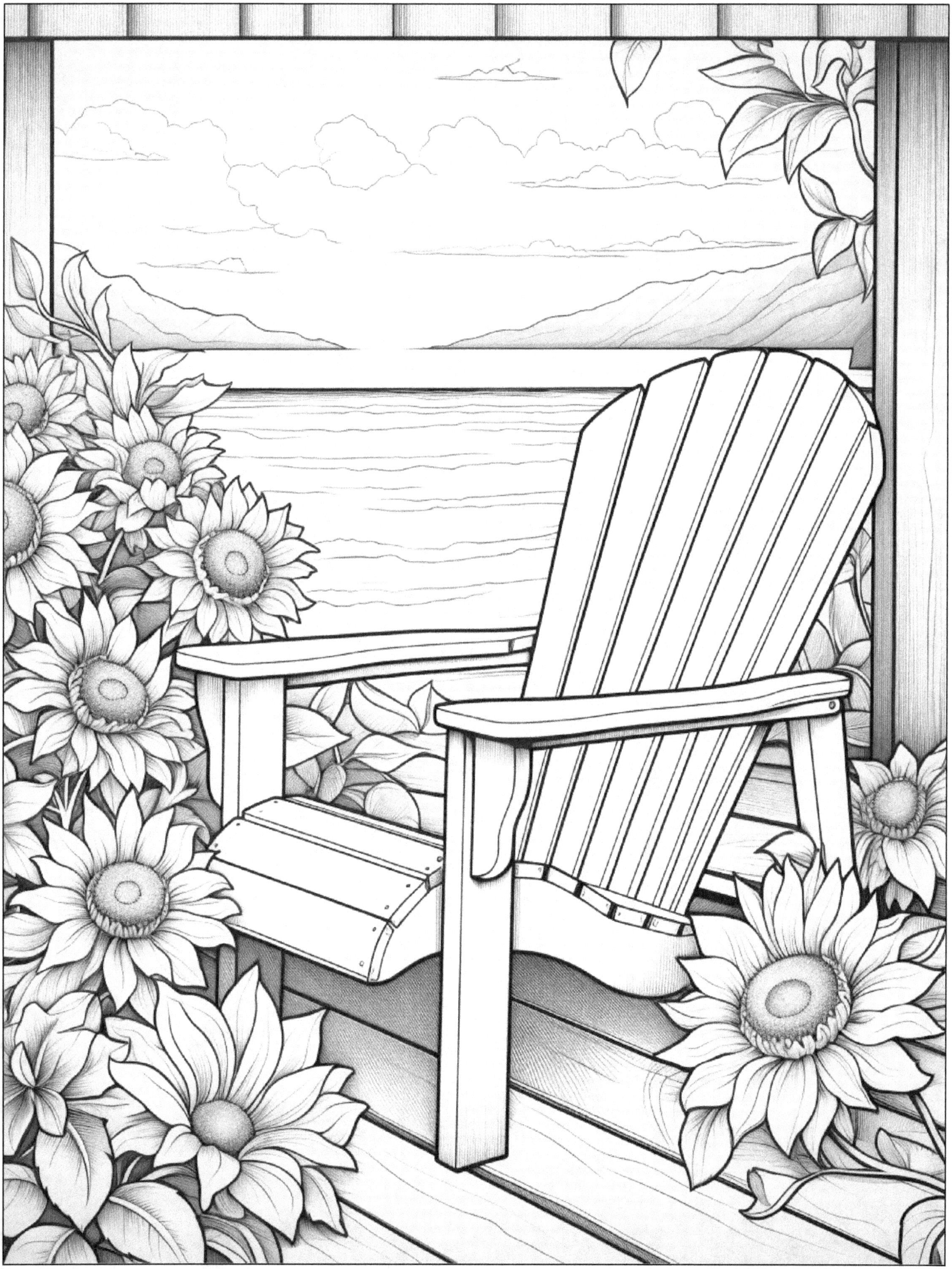

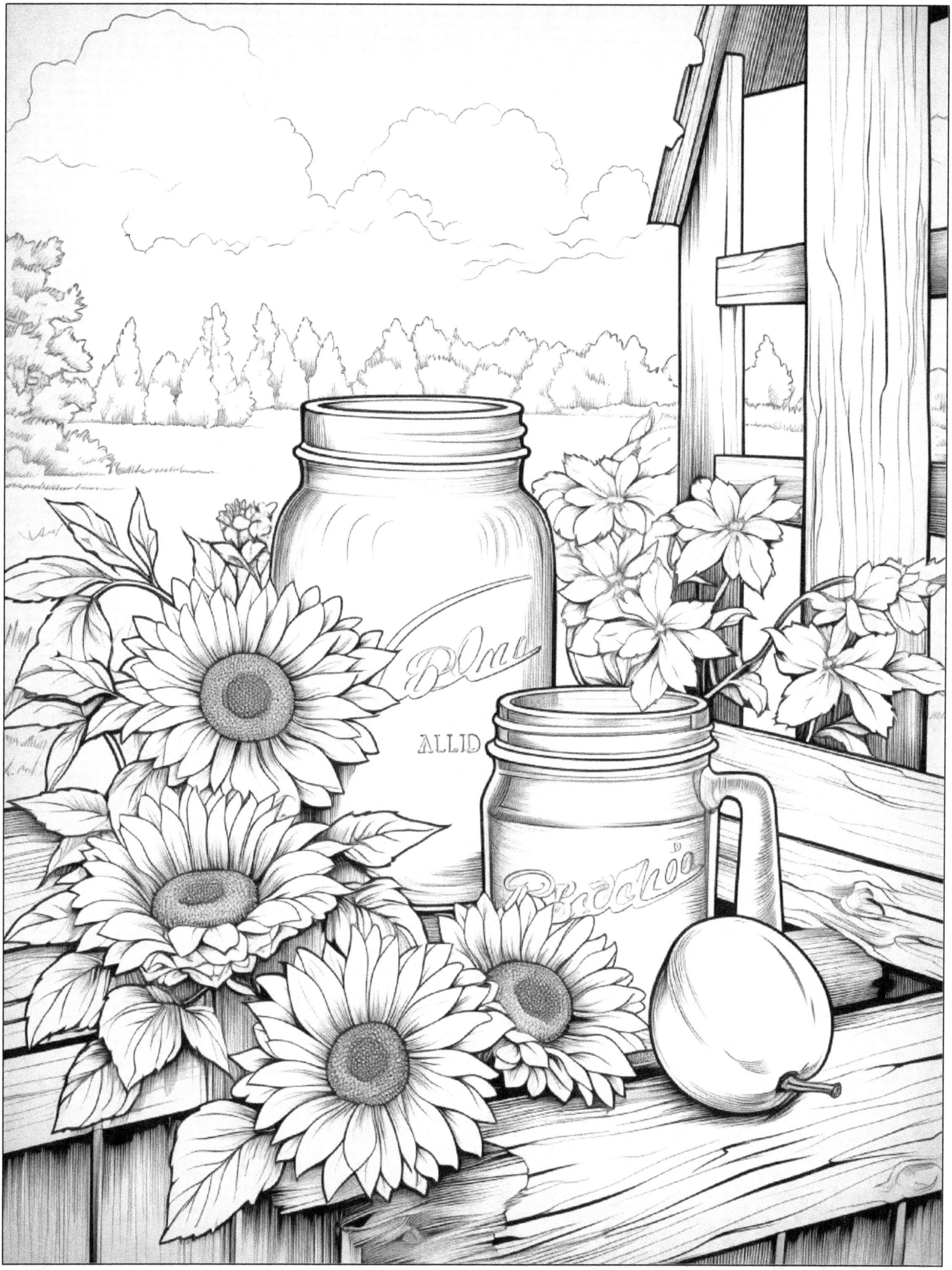
ALLID

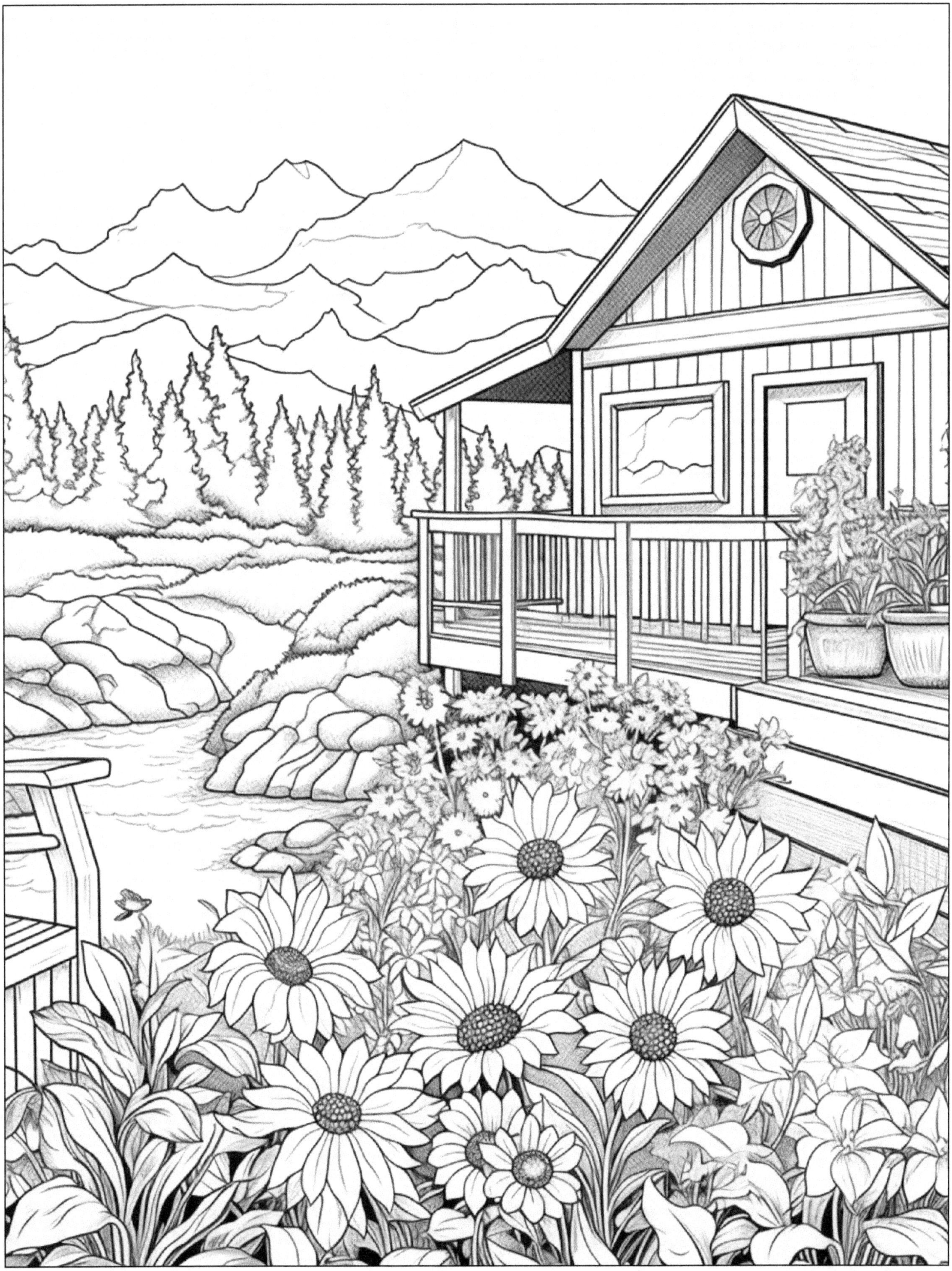

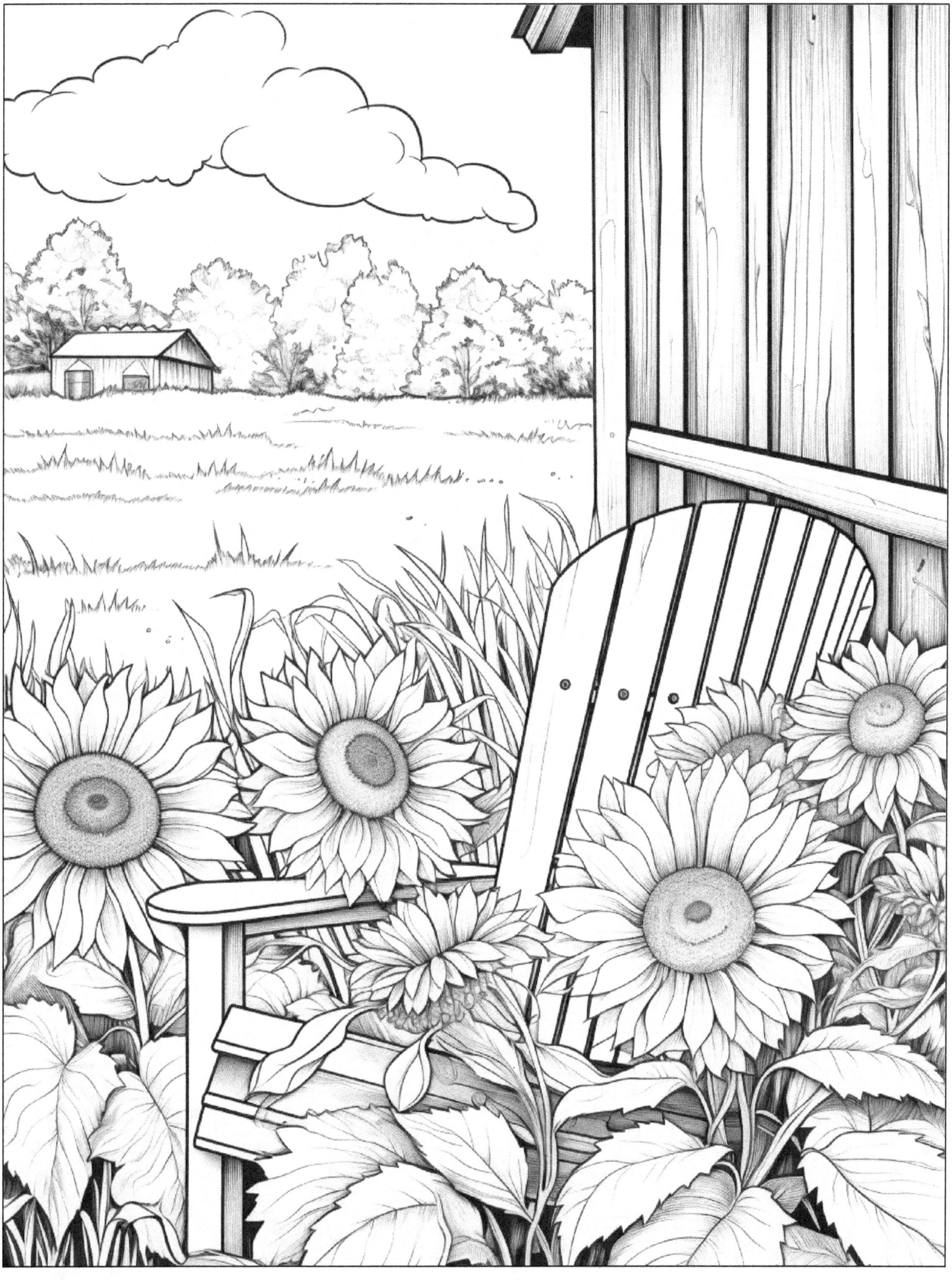

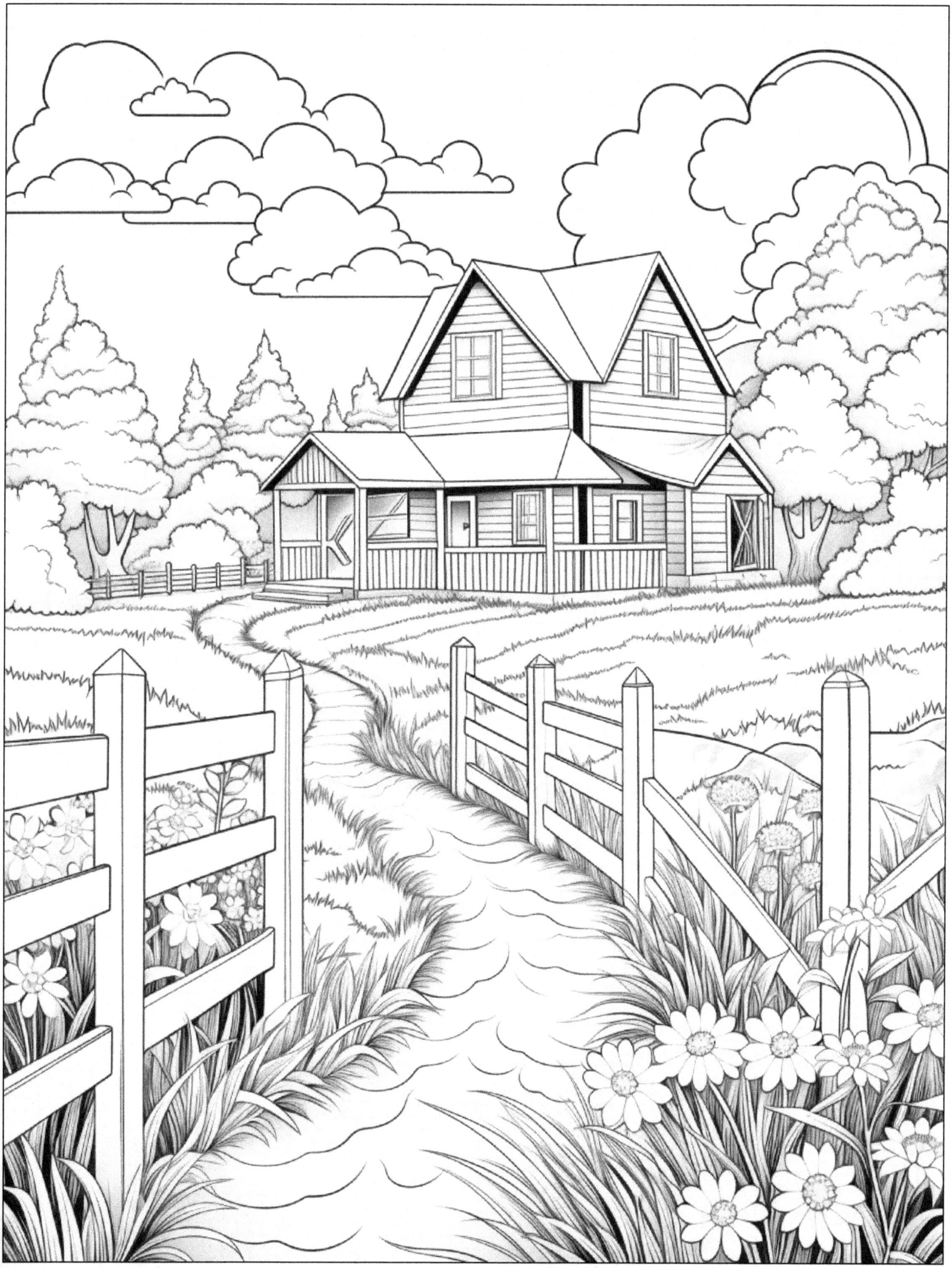

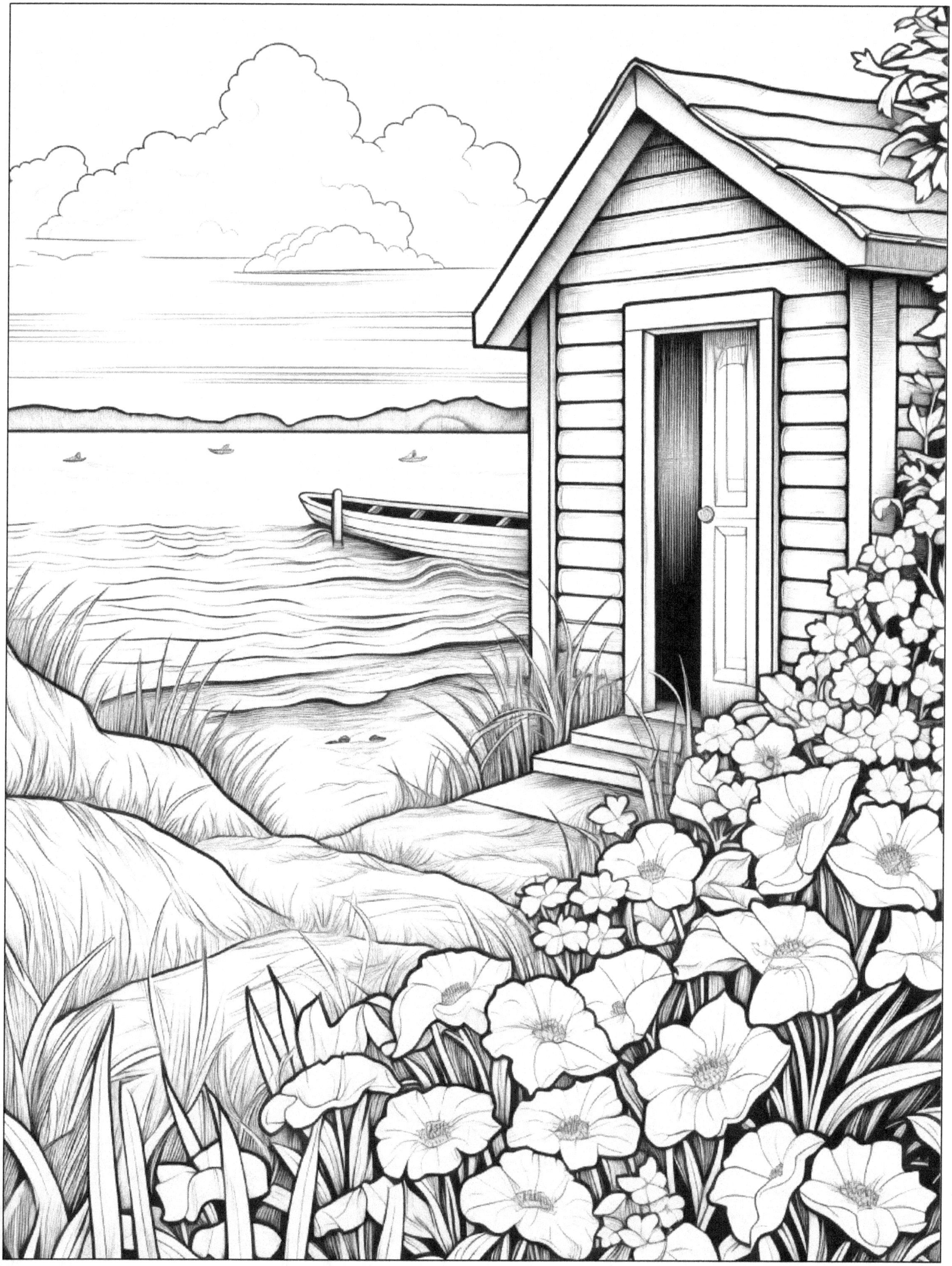

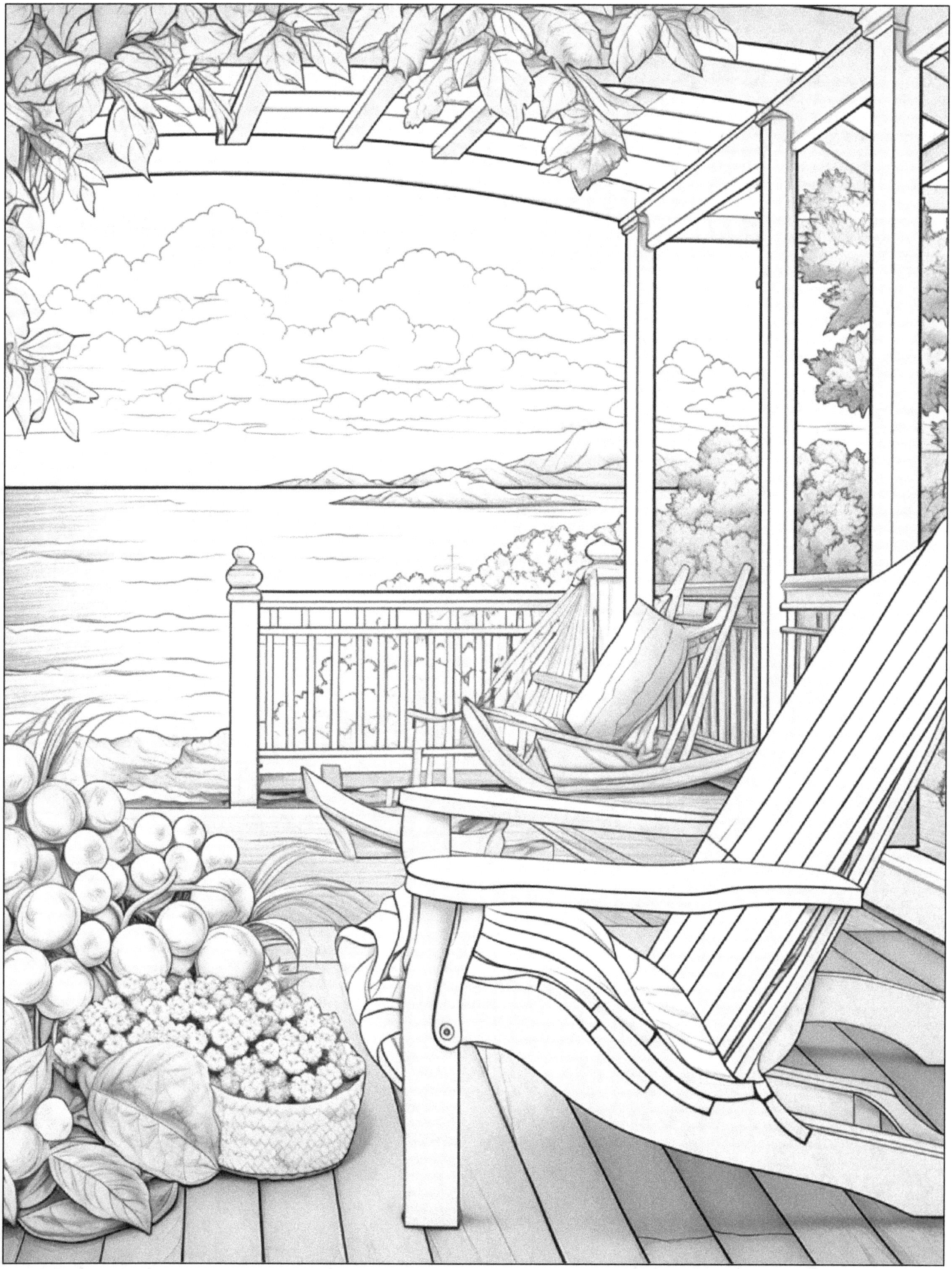

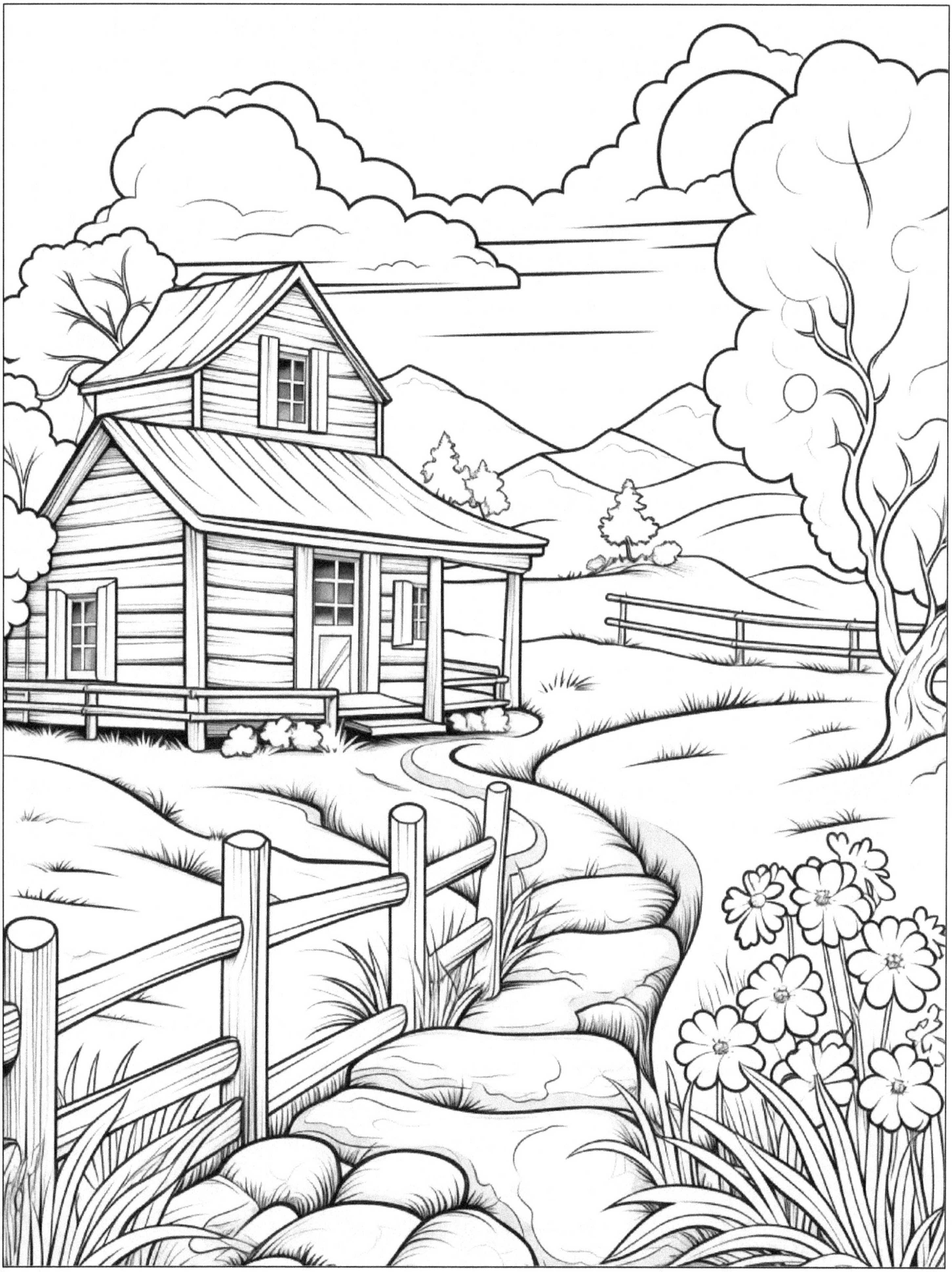

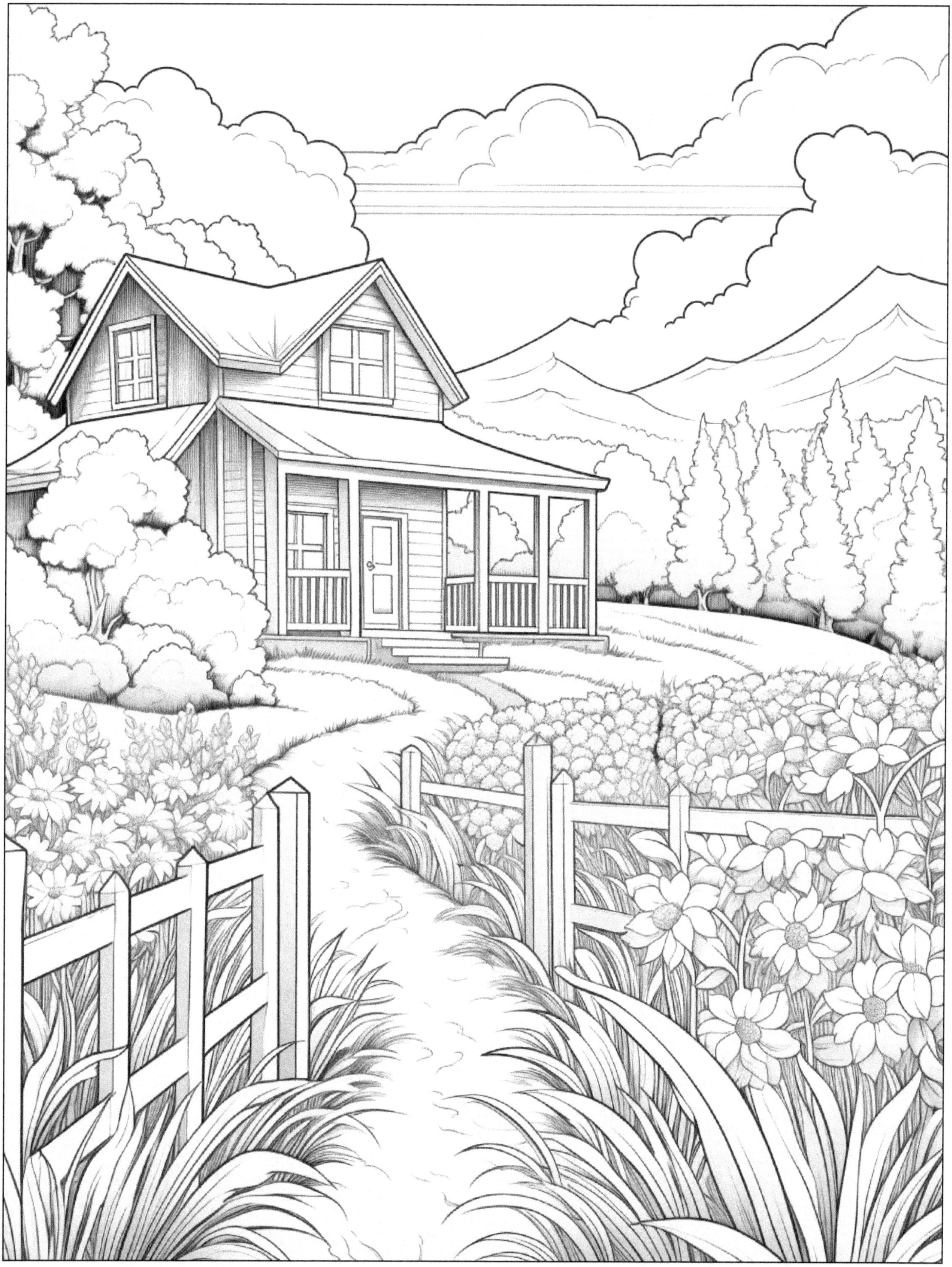

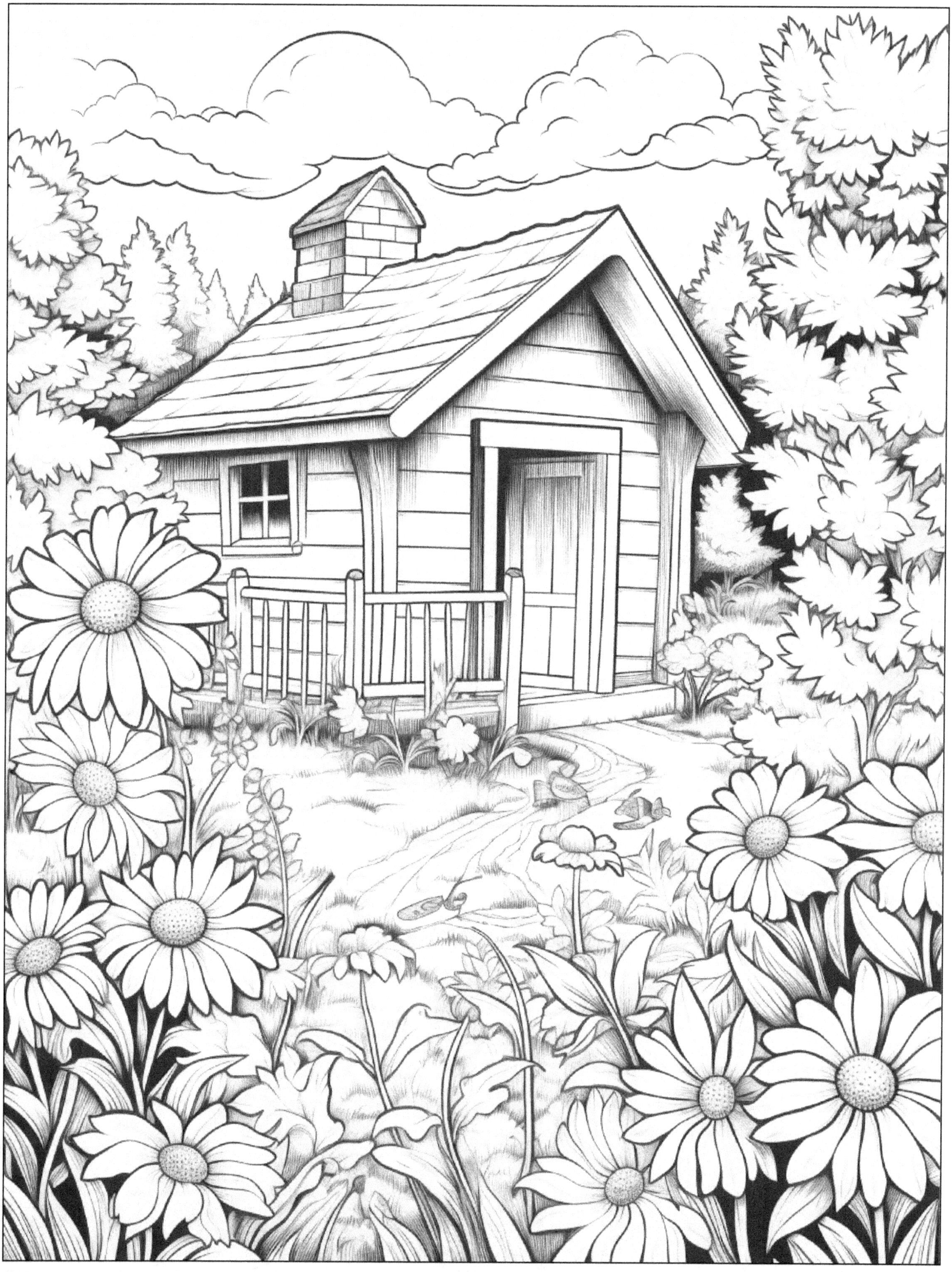

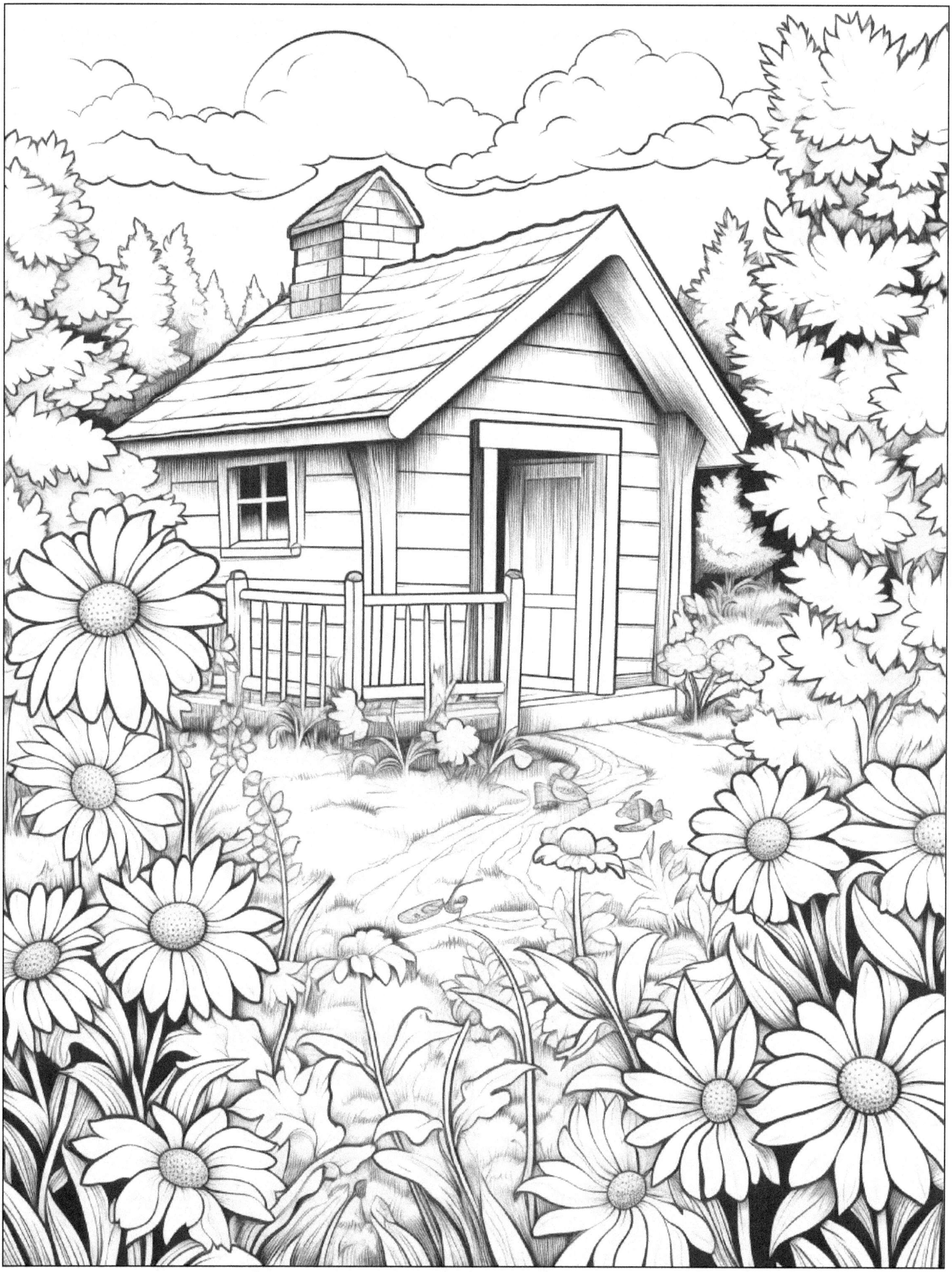

# Thank you

## PLEASE LEAVE US A REVIEW!

IF YOU ENJOYED THIS COLORING BOOK, PLEASE TAKE A MOMENT TO LEAVE A REVIEW. YOUR FEEDBACK HELPS US IMPROVE AND GUIDES OTHER CREATIVE SPIRITS TO THEIR PERFECT COLORING ADVENTURE!

SCAN HERE

www.ingramcontent.com/pod-product-compliance
Lightning Source LLC
Chambersburg PA
CBHW082345220526
45470CB00008B/2654
* 9 7 9 8 3 2 6 4 6 1 1 5 5 *